Kabbalah

Kabbalah

A Very Short Introduction

JOSEPH DAN

OXFORD

UNIVERSITY PRESS

2006

OXFORD
UNIVERSITY PRESS

Oxford University Press, Inc., publishes works that
further Oxford University's objective of excellence
in research, scholarship, and education.

Oxford New York
Auckland Cape Town Dar es Salaam Hong Kong Karachi
Kuala Lumpur Madrid Melbourne Mexico City Nairobi
New Delhi Shanghai Taipei Toronto

With offices in
Argentina Austria Brazil Chile Czech Republic France Greece
Guatemala Hungary Italy Japan Poland Portugal Singapore
South Korea Switzerland Thailand Turkey Ukraine Vietnam

Copyright © 2006 by Joseph Dan

Published by Oxford University Press, Inc.
198 Madison Avenue, New York, NY 10016
www.oup.com

Oxford is a registered trademark of Oxford University Press

Library of Congress Cataloging-in-Publication Data
Dan, Joseph, 1935–
   Kabbalah : a very short introduction / Joseph Dan.
      p. cm.
Includes bibliographical references and index.
ISBN-13: 978-0-19-530034-5
ISBN-10: 0-19-530034-3
1. Cabala   I. Title.
BM525.D355   2005
296.1'6—dc22   2005017169

9 8 7 6 5 4 3 2
Printed in the United States of America
on acid-free paper

Contents

Illustrations

Preface

Every author of a "very short introduction" is faced with the difficult task of finding a way to present his subject in a brief and coherent manner, addressing readers who seek only the basic, yet most important, aspects of the discipline to which the book is dedicated. In the case of the kabbalah, however, there is an added difficulty: many readers will seek in the few pages of this book not only new information, but also a confirmation of their own impression of what the kabbalah is. Some will even, knowingly or unknowingly, seek here a description of what the kabbalah should be. For fifty years I have been trying to respond to the question "what is the kabbalah?" And, in many cases my answer was accepted with disappointment or even resentment: this is not what I believe that the kabbalah is, and certainly it is not what I feel that the kabbalah should be.

The term "kabbalah" has never been used as often and in so many contexts as it is today, yet now, as in the past, it does not have a "real," definite one meaning. From its early beginnings, it has been used in a wide variety of ways. Every medieval kabbalist gave the term his own meaning, which differed slightly or meaningfully from the others. In modern times numerous Jewish and Christian theologians, philosophers, and even scientists have used it in various, sometimes contradictory, ways. It has been an expression of strict Jewish orthodoxy as well as a vehicle for radical, innovative worldviews. The explanation of the meaning of the term must, therefore, be defined within a clear, historical context, stating the time, place, and culture that used it in the past or is using it today. From the point of view of the historian of religious ideas there is no "true" meaning that is above all others. This short introduction is intended, therefore, to present some of the most prominent characteristics of the different phenomena that were described as "kabbalistic" in various periods, countries, and cultural contexts.

Our libraries contain many hundreds of works of kabbalah, printed or still in manuscript form. And, beside these, there are thousands of works—collections of sermons, ethical treatises, and commentaries on the scriptures and the Talmud—that use a little or more kabbalistic terminologies and ideas. As a result, there is hardly a Jewish idea that cannot be described as "kabbalistic" with some justification, as most of these ideas are found in works that use kabbalistic terminology. How can one distinguish between a traditional Jewish ethical norm and a kabbalistic one? Today, it often seems that designating an idea as "kabbalistic" makes it more welcome to outsiders than if it were described as "Jewish." The main work of the medieval kabbalah, the book Zohar, contains 1,400 pages that deal with every conceivable subject. There is nothing that cannot be confirmed by a quotation from the Zohar. A friend of mine who was teaching kabbalah at a university in California in the 1960s produced a beautiful quote from the Zohar to confirm that it is forbidden to study the kabbalah without, at the same time, smoking pot, and he demanded that his students do so in class. I failed in my attempt to persuade him to change his attitude; my authority could not compete with that of the Zohar as he understood it at that time. This small book should therefore be regarded as a subjective selection, augmented by my experience as a historian of religious ideas, of the most prominent meanings attached to the term kabbalah through the ages, without designating any of them as more truthful than the others.

As for the deluge of meanings given to the term in contemporary culture, only a future historian will be able to distinguish between the ephemeral and the enduring ones.

Cambridge, Massachusetts, May 2005

Kabbalah

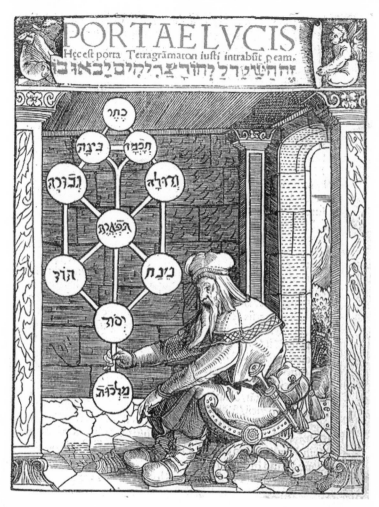

1   A Latin translation of *Shaaey Ora* ("The Gates of Light"), one of
the most influential presentations of the kabbalistic world-view,
written by Joseph Gikatilla in the thirteenth century.

I

Kabbalah:
The Term and Its Meanings

A visitor to the State of Israel is confronted by kabbalah several times every day. When he enters a hotel, he is obligated to face a desk, behind which a large sign reads "Kabbalah"; in English, the same sign reads "Reception." When he purchases anything or pays for a service he receives a piece of paper on which the word "Kabbalah" is written in large Hebrew letters. If there is an English translation on that piece of paper, it reads "Receipt." The term will pop up in scores of contexts. If he is invited to a reception, the Hebrew term for the event is "*kabbalat panim*" (literally, "receiving the face"). If he wishes to visit a bank or a government office he must first check the *kabalat kahal*—the hours in which clerks receive the public, the equivalent of the English "open." Every professor, of any discipline, is engaged every week in a kabbalistic hour, *sheat kabbalah*, that is, office hour, in which his door is open to students. The verb "kbl" is present in every other sentence in Hebrew, meaning simply "to receive." Judging by their behavior, the Hebrew-speaking Israelis seem to be oblivious to the depth of their immersion in mysticism, and treat kabbalah as a simple, mundane word in their language. In a religious context, the key sentence in which this word is used is found in the opening phrase of the talmudic tractate *avot*, one of the most popular rabbinic Hebrew texts, which was probably formulated in the second century CE. The first section of this tractate describes the traditional chain of Jewish law and religious instruction, which was transmitted from generation to generation. The first stage of this transmission, as described in this tractate, is: "Moses received *[kibel]* the Torah on [Mount] Sinai and transmitted it to Joshua, who [transmitted it] to the Elders [of Israel] . . . "; the text goes on to describe the oral transmission of this tradition to the judges, the prophets, and the early sages of the Talmud. This paragraph was used for nearly two thousand years to validate Jewish tradition as a whole, fixing the Mount Sinai revelation as the point of origin, deriving legitimacy from the sanctity of that event. The term "torah" in this sentence was understood to mean everything—scriptures, the law (halakhah), the rules of ethics, the expounding of scriptural verses (midrash)—everything related to truth of divine origin. Some even said that everything that a scholar might innovate was given by God to Moses: what may seem to be an innovative, brilliant religious observation was already known to Moses, informed by God in that all-encompassing revelation. What Moses "received" on that occasion is kabbalah—tradition, which in this context acquired the particular meaning of sacred tradition of divine origin, part of which is found in writing (scriptures), and part transmitted orally from generation to generation by the religious leaders of the Jewish people.

Similar conceptions of tradition are found in Christianity and Islam. The Catholic Church is believed to be the treasury of tradition that gives divine authority to its instructions. Islamic scholars possess, in addition to the Quran, a vast treasure of divine wisdom that was transmitted orally from Muhammad to his disciples and their disciples. In Hebrew, this tradition is called *masoret* ("that which has been transmitted") or kabbalah ("that which has been received"). The word "kabbalah," in such contexts, is an abbreviation, indicating divine truth received by Moses from God; the term does not refer to a particular kind of content. It describes origin and the manner of transmission, without emphasizing any discipline or subject. Essentially, this term conveys the opposite of what usually is recognized as "mysticism," which is conceived as relating to original, individual visions and experiences. "Kabbalah" in the Hebrew religious vocabulary means nonindividual, nonexperiential religious truth, which is received by tradition.

The Term in the Middle Ages

This was the only religious meaning of the term "kabbalah" for a full millennium. In the thirteenth century, a variant was added to it. Groups of Jewish esoterics and mystics, mainly in Spain, Provence, and later Italy, claimed to be in possession of a secret tradition concerning the meaning of the scriptures and other ancient texts, expounding them as relating to dynamic processes within the divine realms. Their origins and teachings will be discussed in some detail in the next chapters. They presented themselves as different in some ways from their coreligionists, and described themselves using several terms. Among these terms we find self-congratulatory ones such as "*maskilim*" ("those in the know") and "*nakdanim*" ("those who know the secrets of language"), among others. A prevalent one was "*yodeey hen*"—"those who know the secret wisdom," that is, *hochmah nisteret* ("secret lore"). Yet another of these terms was "*mekubalim*," meaning "those who possess a secret tradition," in addition to the usual kabbalah, which is known to everybody. In the following decades, the terms "kabbalah" and "kabbalists" became the dominant names for these groups, though they did not completely replace other appellations. The term "kabbalah" in this context means an additional layer of tradition, one that does not replace anything in the usual, exoteric tradition but adds to it an esoteric stratum. This secret tradition, so the kabbalists believed and claimed, was received by Moses on Mount Sinai directly from God, and was secretly transmitted from generation to generation up to the present. Most of this transmission, they claimed, was oral, given from father to son and from teacher to his disciples.

3

The word "kabbalah" is, therefore, a claim by Jewish spiritualists from the High Middle Ages to this day that they have a tradition that was held secret for many centuries. This is a self-designation that denies creativity and originality. These people just happened to receive these secrets from the previous generation, or happened to find manuscripts that contain these teachings. In a few extraordinary cases, people claimed to have learned these secrets in a visionary way, by the spirit of prophecy or by uplifting their souls to the divine world and participating in the deliberations of the celestial academy or by meeting a supernal messenger, an angel or a divine power or, sometimes, a prophet such as Elijah, who revealed these secrets to them. Even in these cases we do not find the kabbalists saying that what was revealed to them is new or original. Even in the few examples in which the way the kabbalah was transmitted was supernatural, the content and the teachings were regarded as ancient and traditional. It is inconceivable, from the point of view of the kabbalists, that a medieval or modern spiritualist is able to possess knowledge that was not known, in greater depth and detail, by King Solomon, the Prophet Isaiah, and the talmudic sages. Divine truth is eternal, and it is shared by everybody who is worthy of it, and the nearer one is to the source of tradition, that is, the revelation on Mount Sinai, the more complete and profound the knowledge. One can only learn more through the discovery of more ancient books, or studying in greater depth the old sources. The kabbalah, according to the kabbalists, is never new; it can be newly discovered or newly received, but essentially it is millennia-old divine truth.

Scholars, of course, hold the opposite view. From the point of view of historians of ideas and historians of religion, the kabbalah is a new phenomenon, which first appeared in southern Europe in the last decades of the twelfth century. It is the result of original thought and the fruit of the individual creativity of each kabbalist (though they usually have ancient sources on which to rely, as will be discussed in detail below). While the kabbalists insist that the kabbalah is one truth, even when expressed in different terms and styles, scholars view each kabbalist as an original writer, who expresses his own worldview, which may differ much or little from those of other kabbalists. For historians, there is no "kabbalah" in the singular. There are the kabbalahs of the Provence school and the Girona school, the kabbalah of Moses de Leon in thirteenth-century Spain, and that of Isaac Luria in sixteenth-century Safed. Modern kabbalists wrote extensive works dedicated to showing that the teachings of Luria are identical to those of the Zohar. Historians tend to emphasize the individuality and uniqueness of kabbalist's writings. At the same time, it is legitimate to look for some underlying similarities that are found in most (never in all) kabbalistic expressions, which characterize the discipline as a whole. Yet, one should be very careful when drawing such conclusions concerning the common denominators to many kabbalistic systems: sometimes similarities are more apparent than real. The writers come from the same religious culture; read the same books; use the same terminology, which is regarded as authentic and authoritative; read each other's writings; and often imitate their predecessors' styles, but their writings actually convey different meanings. Modern writers who emphasize the antiquity of the kabbalah and the uniformity of its basic ideas are, in fact, trying to validate and uphold the claims of the kabbalists rather than to study their works in a critical, historical manner.

Expansion of the Meanings of Kabbalah

The Hebrew terms relating to Jewish religious culture usually retained their original meaning when used in other languages and different cultural contexts. Terms such as "halakhah," "Talmud," "midrash," "mitzvot," "Hasidism," and many others have been compared to phenomena in other religions, but their Jewish context has never been denied or diminished. The fate of the word "kabbalah" has been entirely different. Looking at the meanings of this term in the last five hundred years, it seems that many of its uses could not—and still cannot—be accepted as an aspect of Jewish religious culture. There is no "Christian Hasidism" and no "Islamic Talmud," yet kabbalah has been identified, insistently, with Christian and universal spiritual phenomena. Kabbalah has been described as Gnosticism, Jewish or non-Jewish, even by the best scholars who have studied it, from Heinrich Graetz, who opposed it, to Gershom Scholem, who presented it as the intrinsic spiritual force within Judaism. Count Giovani Pico dela Mirandola and his followers in Renaissance Italy described it as the ultimate expression of magic; the essence of Greek philosophy, especially that of Pythagoras; and, above all, the most important source for the Christian religion. Needless to say, it has been identified as mysticism, by friend and foe alike. It has been conceived as expressing universal spiritual aspirations that do not distinguish between nations, cultures, or religions. The adjective "kabbalistic" has been applied in every conceivable and unconceivable context. A modern scholar in Finland (Simo Parpola) discovered it in ancient Assyrian religion. It is a meaningful, even central, component of the New Age worldview. Carl Gustav Jung saw in it universal archetypes of the human psyche, and its influences have been identified in the writings of European philosophers, mystics, and scientists of the seventeenth and eighteenth centuries, from Giordano Bruno to Gottfried Leibnitz. The Yale University literary critic Harold Bloom equated it with literary criticism and found its influence throughout modern literature and philosophy. It has been used as a synonym for mysticism and magic, and for spirituality in general.

Some of these meanings may contain important elements of truth, yet it should be pointed out that no other postbiblical Jewish term or concept has been universalized in a similar manner. Very few non-Jewish thinkers claim that the Talmud has a universal message for all cultures and religions; this is said about the kabbalah alone among the many aspects of Jewish religiosity. It has been so thoroughly accepted within European culture that even the derogatory, negative meanings attached to it have not diminished its universal appeal. The term has been used to denote secret, dark, and evil intentions ("cabal" in English) and has been identified with superstition and irrationality, yet it remains a meaningful component of European culture. Even when it is evil and harmful, the kabbalah is still regarded as too good to be left to the Jews alone.

The meanings of the term "kabbalah" have also multiplied in Hebrew and Jewish contexts since the sixteenth century. The most important new meaning is the increasing significance of the magical in the concept of the kabbalah. The flourishing of hagiographic literature since the sixteenth century describing the employs of medieval and contemporary scholars and leaders contributed to this. Legends about figures such as Maimonides (who was not a kabbalist) and Nachmanides (who was) described them working miracles by the power of the magical secrets of the kabbalah. Even today, people who seek religious authority in Israel are sometimes described, by themselves or by others, as "kabbalists," when the term usually denotes not spiritual aspirations or knowledge of celestial processes but rather magical faculties. A blessing given by someone who is reputed to be a "kabbalist" is regarded as especially effective among many orthodox Jews. Sometimes this is the result of the application of the term "kabbalah ma'asit," meaning magical tradition, to the kabbalah in general. In current Israeli Hebrew, "kabbalist" and "magician" have almost the exact same meaning.

So what is the kabbalah really? There is no answer to this question. Few people will say that it is the essence of Assyrian religion, while many will say that it is the essence of Christianity. Almost everybody will identify it as mysticism, and many will see it as a secret magical tradition. A common denominator, I believe, of answers to the question "What is kabbalah?" is that the kabbalah is something that I have a vague notion of, but somebody, somewhere, knows exactly what it means.

The role of the historian of ideas is not to uncover what something "really" is, but to present the development of a concept's meanings in different historical and cultural contexts, seeking to determine as far as possible the many usages and definitions that it has acquired throughout its history. It is not the task of the historian to state that Gershom Scholem was right and Simo Parpola is wrong or vice versa. It is not his task to declare that Johannes Reuchlin was "really" a kabbalist and Carl Jung was not. It is a historical fact that in the last half millennium hundreds of thinkers used the term in different ways, departing from the cultural context in which the kabbalah emerged. The story of this process has to be told in historical terms, avoiding the designation of one meaning as more "true" than the others.

Kabbalah and Mysticism

Until the nineteenth century, there were no Jewish or Muslim "mystics." The term "mysticism" is completely absent from Jewish and Islamic cultures, and there is no counterpart in Hebrew or Arabic to the term and the concept it represents. The concept of mysticism as an aspect of religious spirituality grew in Christianity, and there were numerous Christian thinkers who described themselves, or others, as mystics. The meaning of the term is thus derived from what a scholar may see as the central aspect or common denominator of the ideas and experiences that Christians described as mystical. In the same way, terms derived from this central idea of mysticism—such *via mystica*, the mystical way of life, prayer, and devotion that leads to *unio mystica*, the mystical union with God—are understood according to their authentic usage within the development of Christian spirituality. Naturally, definitions and meanings will differ according to the scholar's identification of what is mystical within the Christian tradition. Using this term to describe Jewish (or Muslim) phenomena is therefore an analogy, based on one's acquaintance with Christian mysticism. It is actually a statement that this or that Jewish or Muslim religious phenomenon is similar to another one that in a Christian context has been described as mystical.

In present-day scholarship there is a tendency to identify Christian mysticism in terms of the attitude toward language. Most traditional definitions of mysticism describe it as the aspiration—and, sometimes, the achievement—of a direct, experiential relationship with God, seeking union with the divine. There were, however, two related flaws in this traditional approach: most of the characteristics assigned to mysticism were valid also to religion in general, thus portraying mysticism as "religion, only a little more so." This traditional approach also presented the relationship between religion and mysticism as a quantitative rather than qualitative one, while most mystics insisted that their experiences were essentially different from those of their co-religionists. A unique characteristic of mysticism that is opposed, in most cases, to ordinary religious experience is the denial of language's ability to express religious truth. While religion is an expression of faith in the words of scripture and revelation, mystics tend to claim that truth lies beyond any possibility of expression by terms derived from sensual experience or logical deduction. Linguistic communication is understood through the sensual and logical messages that language conveys. If mystics see these realms as irrelevant to mystical truth, language cannot serve to communicate supernal truth. Some opaque, imprecise hints at the mysteries of the divine may be conveyed by various methods using words, but these should not be taken literally. In mysticism, language is apophatic, a "language of unsaying," language that denies its own communicative message. In this way, mysticism and religion are different spiritual phenomena, separated by their opposing conceptions of linguistic communication.

This is a purely negative description, suggesting what the mystics do not believe in rather than what they positively hold to be their unique religious expression. Yet it serves as a basis to explore the particular characteristics of each historical phenomenon that we wish to designate as "mystical." The universal, distinctive aspect of mysticism is its denial of the senses, logic, and communicative language as avenues leading to the knowledge and understanding of the divine. The positive aspects are dependent on particular historical, cultural, and spiritual contexts, which give every expression of mysticism its unique character.

When the term "mysticism" was applied to Jewish (and Muslim) spiritual phenomena, many scholars believed that they have discovered a parallel to Christian mysticism: the esoteric, mysterious literature of the kabbalah. It became common to identify the kabbalah with mysticism, as if the term was just a Hebrew word for the familiar Christian phenomenon. In a similar way, the Muslim Sufi literature was designated as "Islamic mysticism." These generalizations are mostly invalid. Sufism and kabbalah are phenomena that each developed in particular cultural and spiritual circumstances that have very little in common with the emergence of Christian mysticism. The concept of ancient tradition that permeates the kabbalah, and the sack that early Islamic Sufis wore, which probably gave them this appellation, have no parallel in Christian mysticism. Yet it is a fact that when one seeks Jewish candidates for the mantle of "mystic" in an analogical manner, one may find several such examples among the kabbalists. If the tendency to seek a realm of divine truth that is beyond the senses, logic, and language is a universal one to be found among the adherents of every spiritual structure (though the number of such people may be exceedingly small), it is natural that the Jewish representatives of this tendency will be found among the esoteric circles of the kabbalists. This does not mean that all kabbalists are mystics. It means only that people who had such inclinations found a haven among the kabbalists. Many kabbalists were first and foremost exegetes, preachers, theologians, and traditionalists, but among them we can identify some mystics, using the criteria derived from Christian mysticism and applying them, analogically, to the Jewish cultural context.

2

Ancient Jewish Mysticism and the Emergence of the Kabbalah

The various schools of the kabbalists, from the late twelfth century to the present, are just one—though undoubtedly a most prominent and influential one—of the manifestations of esotericism and mysticism in Jewish religious culture. At least two major groups of Jewish spiritualists demonstrated very similar attitudes to the kabbalists, though they knew nothing about the kabbalah and its specific terminologies and worldviews.

The beginning of Jewish esotericism can be found in a talmudic statement, in the Mishnah (Hagiga 2:1), originating probably from the first century CE. It declares that it is forbidden to expound two sections in the scriptures in public, and warns of the danger in studying them even in small groups. The first section is the chapters of the Book of Genesis, describing the creation of the cosmos, which is called in the Talmud *ma'aseh bereshit* (the work of genesis). The second section is the first chapter of the Book of Ezekiel, called the *ma'aseh merkavah* (the work of the chariot), the description of Ezekiel's vision of the celestial chariot in Ezekiel 1 and 10. Thus, these chapters and subjects were separated from the body of Jewish traditional expounding and speculation, and relegated to a separate realm, which was regarded as spiritually—and sometimes even physically—dangerous.

ספר יצירה

I D E S T.

LIBER IEZIRAH

Qui

ABRAHAMO PATRIARCHÆ
adſcribitur, unà cum Commentario Rabi ABRAHAM
F. D. ſuper 32 Semitis Sapientiæ, à quibus liber
IEZIRAH incipit.

Tranſlatus & Notis illuſtratus à

JOANNE STEPHANO RITTANGELIO
Ling. Orient. in Elect. Acad. Regiomontanæ
Prof. Extraord.

AMSTELODAMI,
APUD IOANNEM & IODOCUM IANSSONIOS,
M. DC. XLII.

2 The ancient *Sefer Yezira*, the Book of Creation, describes the
process of creation mainly by the power of the letters of the alphabet.
(Latin translation, Amsterdam 1642).

The talmudic sages discuss this prohibition in detail and give examples of the problems and the dangers of these scriptures, often using opaque, mystifying language. One of the best-known parables attached to this prohibition is the story of the four sages who entered a *pardes*—a royal garden. (The word *"pardes"* is derived from Persian, and its Greek form was adopted by European languages as Paradise.) Of these four well-known talmudic figures one died as the result of this experience, the second went out of his mind, the third became a heretic, and only one—Rabbi Akibah ben Joseph—"entered in peace and came out in peace." The text does not explain what the "entrance to the *pardes*" actually means, but it was understood to represent a profound religious experience of entering the divine realm and suggesting some kind of a meeting with God. There are numerous discussions of these subjects in rabbinic literature of late antiquity, and these three terms—*ma'aseh bereshit*, *ma'aseh merkavah*, and *pardes*—became central in the language of Jewish esoterics, spiritualists, and mystics over the next two millennia.

Ancient Esoteric Treatises

A small library of about two dozen treatises reached us from the writings of Jewish esoterics in late antiquity dealing with these two subjects, the secret of creation and the secret of the divine realm, the *merkavah*. It is known as the "Hekhalot [celestial palaces or temples] and Merkavah" literature, because several of the treatises have these terms in their titles. This literature deals with four main subjects: the first is that of cosmology and cosmogony, detailed descriptions of the process of creation and the ways in which God directs the universe (including the structure of paradise and hell, and several astronomical discussions). The most detailed work in this group is Seder Rabba de-Bereshit (The Extended Description of Genesis). The second main subject in this small library is magic.

These treatises include the most elaborate ancient Jewish directory for magical formulas—Harba de-Moshe (The Sword of Moses), a list of several hundred magical incantations and procedures, dealing in many subjects from medical remedies to love potions to walking on water. Magic is a prominent subject in several other treatises in this literature, especially in Sefer ha-Razim (The Book of Secrets). The third main subject is expounding the description of the chariot in Ezekiel and other biblical sections describing the abode of God. Thus, for instance, in Reuyot Yehezkel (The Visions of Ezekiel), Ezekiel is described as having envisioned seven chariots reflected in the waters of the river Kvar. These texts include detailed angelological lists, naming the angels and their functions, as well as presentations of the secret names of God and of the archangels.

The fourth subject—found only in about five of these treatises—is meaningfully different from the others: it describes an active procedure by which a person can ascend to the divine realms and reach the highest level, and even "face God in his glory." This process of ascension is called in these texts, paradoxically, "descent to the chariot," and the sages who do it are called *yordey ha-merkavah* (the descenders to the chariot). This practice is attributed in these texts to the two great sages of the early talmudic period, Rabbi Akibah and Rabbi Ishmael. Unlike the vast talmudic-midrashic literature and most of the Hekhalot and Merkavah treatises, these texts do not rely on expounding biblical verses (midrash), but relate direct, personal spiritual experiences. The claim for veracity does not rely on "the verse said," as is usual in most Hebrew postbiblical literature, but on personal experience—"I saw," "I heard," "I envisioned." They used terminology that is not found anywhere else, such as the term "*hekhalot*" in the plural, indicating the seven palaces or temples that are situated, one above the other and one inside the other in the seventh, highest heaven. The sages who overcome the many dangers on the elaborate way of ascension join with the angels in the celestial rituals of praise to God. Unlike any other ancient texts, these treatises abound with hymns of praise to God, some of which are recited by angels and others said by the *yordey ha-merkavah* themselves. There are many different definitions of mysticism; I am not aware of one that would not include the descenders to the chariot as an excellent example of mysticism.

One of these treatises, probably connected with the group of *yordey ha-merkavah* but without making use of this term, had particular influence on the history of Jewish esotericism and mysticism. It is called Shiur Komah (The Measurement of the Height). This short work, attributed to Rabbi Akibah and Rabbi Ishmael, seems to be an intensely anthropomorphic description of God. It does not relate a divine experience; its core is a list of God's limbs, beard, forehead, eyes, and irises (derived mainly from the description of the lover in Song of Songs 5:10–16), each of which is designated by a series of obscure, strange, unpronounceable names, and each is measured in terms of miles, feet, and fingers. The author defines the measurements he uses, and the basic one is the length of the whole universe (based on Isaiah 40:12); each divine limb is trillions of times longer than this basic measurement. It is possible that this anthropomorphic text is actually a polemic against more radical views that derived from the Song of Songs simplistic human descriptions of God. Be that as it may, for Jewish esoteric tradition, the Shiur Komah defined the standard image of God for the next millennium and a half. Its impact was enormous, and the kabbalistic system of the divine attributes, the *sefirot*, is described in terms from the Shiur Komah.

Sefer Yezira, the Book of Creation

One of the most important sources for medieval kabbalistic terminology is an ancient nonkabbalistic treatise entitled Sefer Yezira (The Book of Creation). It is often regarded, erroneously, as the earliest work of the kabbalah. In fact, Sefer Yezira is a cosmological, scientific treatise that describes the process of creation mainly by the power of the letters of the alphabet, and presents an early Jewish conception of grammar. It appeared in Jewish culture in the tenth century, when Jewish rationalistic philosophers and scientists, headed by Rav Saadia Gaon in Babylonia, Dunash Ibn Tamim, and Shabbatai Donolo, wrote commentaries on the text, using it to present their own scientific systems of cosmology, anthropology, and psychology. It is evident that in the tenth century it was regarded as an ancient work, and the multiplicity and complexity of its versions proves that it had developed and was edited for several generations before its appearance. The date of its origin is unknown. Some scholars suggest it is a first century work, written before the destruction of Jerusalem in 70 CE, while others maintain that it was written in the ninth century, under the influence of Islamic culture. Most scholars assume that it was written in the third or fourth century, but no definite proof can be presented for any of these possibilities. There are scores of different versions of the work, and the first comprehensive scholarly edition was published recently by the scholar Peter Hayman. The concluding sentences of the treatise describe Abraham as knowing the secrets of this work, and because of this it has traditionally been ascribed to Abraham the Patriarch. Between the tenth and the twelfth centuries it was interpreted by rationalists and scientists, but in the second half of the twelfth century it was adopted by esoterics, mystics, and kabbalists, and has been identified with this aspect of Jewish religious culture since that time.

The work presents a system of cosmogony and cosmology that seems to be deliberately different from the one described in the Book of Genesis and in the detailed interpretations of that narrative in traditional rabbinic sources, including the Talmud and midrash. It cites no authority, and rarely relies on biblical verses. The book does not use the traditional Hebrew term for creation, "*bara*"; the dominant verbs are "hewed" and "crafted" (*haqaq*, *hazav*, and *yazar*). The universe was hewed, according to the first paragraph, by thirty-two "wondrous paths of wisdom," and engraved in "three books." The "paths" are described as ten *sefirot* and the twenty-two letters of the Hebrew alphabet. These *sefirot* are not divine powers; thirteenth-century kabbalists did not attribute this meaning to this term. The *sefirot* are described as the directions or dimensions of the cosmos (north, south, east, west, up, down, beginning, end, good, and evil), as well as the holy beasts of Ezekiel's chariot, the stages of the emergence of the three elements (divine spirit, air or wind, and water and fire), and other characteristics that are unclear. The early commentators interpreted the *sefirot* as the ten basic numbers from one to ten. Most of the work is dedicated to a detailed description how the various letters and groups of letters served the process of creation and dominate the various aspects of the universe.

The central concept presented in this work is *harmonia mundi* (harmony of the universe). There are three layers of existence, the cosmic, that of time, and that of man. Each letter, or group of letters, is in charge of one aspect of each layer. Thus, for instance, the Hebrew letters that can be pronounced in two different ways—whose number, according to this work, is seven—in the cosmos, are in charge of the seven planets; in "time," are in charge of the seven days of the week; and, in man, are in charge of the seven orifices in the head (eyes, ears, nostrils, and mouth). The twelve letters that the author describes as "simple" are in charge of the twelve zodiac signs, the twelve months, and the twelve principal limbs, and so on. This model was used by subsequent thinkers to develop the concept of human beings as microcosmos, reflecting the characteristics of the cosmos as a whole (especially by Shabbatai Donolo, who used it to interpret the verse in Genesis 1:27, indicating that man was created in the image of God). God achieved the process of creation by tying "crowns" to the letters and assigning them to rule their particular realms in these three layers. The harmony that results from the same linguistic power governing the three realms was accepted, in different ways, by subsequent Jewish thinkers and served as a central concept in the kabbalistic worldview.

The concept that the universe was created by the power of divine speech is an ancient one in Judaism, and the Sefer Yezira developed this idea systematically. The guiding principle seems to have been that if creation is accomplished by language, then the laws of creation are the laws of language. Grammar thus was conceived as the basic law of nature. The author developed a Hebrew grammar based on 231 "roots"—the number of possible combinations of 22 letters. He explained the existence of good and evil in the universe as a grammatical process: if the letter *ayin* is added to the "root" *ng* as a prefix, it gives *ong*, great pleasure, but if it is added as a suffix, it means infliction, malady. The author also insisted that everything in the universe, following grammatical principles, has two aspects, parallel to the gender duality of masculine and feminine.

The work—as far as can be gleaned from the sections that are common to the main versions—seems to be mainly scientific. It does not mention the people of Israel, nor any religious concept—the Sabbath, commandments, ethics, redemption, messiah, afterlife, sin, sanctity, or anything of this kind. It is no wonder that editors of various versions and early and late commentators tried to insert into the text and into their interpretation elements of Jewish religiosity. The fact that the kabbalists gave new meaning to the terminology of the Sefer Yezira, and scores of them wrote commentaries on this treatise, positioned this work in the heart of Jewish sacred tradition, a source of divine secret wisdom parallel to that of the Hebrew Bible.

The Pietists of Medieval Germany

In the High Middle Ages, a short time before the emergence of the kabbalah, we find another example of a major Jewish school of estoerics and mystics, centered mainly in the Rhineland, known as Hasidey Ashkenaz, the pietists of Germany. Most writers of this school, and many of the leaders, writers, halakhists, and poets of German Jewry in twelfth and thirteenth century, belonged to one family, the Kalonymus family. The central figures were Rabbi Judah ben Samuel the Pious (who died in 1217), and his relative and disciple, Rabbi Eleazar ben Judah of Worms (who died about 1230). Their worldview was deeply influence by the waves of crusaders who massacred Jews in France, Germany, and England on their way to fight the Muslims in the Holy Land. They developed a unique system of religious ethics, directed to prepare their people for the experience of martyrdom (*kiddusch ha-shem*).

We have about a score of volumes, many of which are still in manuscripts, in which the pietists presented an esoteric worldview that was deeply pessimistic about the nature of the created world. They saw the world mainly as a series of trials presented by God in order to prepare the few righteous, courageous people for everlasting bliss in the next world. One of the most important ideas they presented and expounded is that the divine world consists of several layers, each emanating from the superior one. The tasks of making revelations to prophets and receiving human prayers were relegated to secondary divine powers, which emanated from the eternal, perfect, and unchanging Godhead. We have several, independent descriptions of a system of emanated divine powers (often three in number) from the pietists and other circles of esoterics. Rabbi Judah the Pious developed a unique conception of the Hebrew prayers, intensely mystical in character, which viewed the text of the traditional prayers as a reflection of a hidden, intrinsic numerical harmony that binds together the words and letters of the sacred texts and all phenomena of existence.

The writings of these circles of esoterics are presented, in most cases, as commentaries on biblical verses, which serve as the source of authority for the speculations included in them. We do not know of any practical, active aspect of these esoteric speculations. They used the Hekhalot and Merkavah texts extensively, but we do not know of any attempt to follow the visionary, experiential path described by the descenders to the chariot. They did incorporate the image of the Shiur Komah as one of the divine emanated powers.

The early circles of the kabbalists were very similar to the Kalonymus family circle and the other groups of esoterics in medieval Germany. The earliest manifestations of the kabbalah are, first, an anonymous work, the Book Bahir, which was written in Provence or northern Spain around 1185; second, a circle of kabbalists in Provence, the most prominent figure of which was Rabbi Isaac ben Abraham the Blind; and third, a school of kabbalists that flourished in Girona, in Catalonia, in the first half of the thirteenth century. The Girona kabbalists, whose most prominent leader was Rabbi Moses ben Nachman (Nachmanides), integrated the teachings of the Book Bahir with those of the Provence school, expounded and developed them, and established the basic ideas and terms that characterized the kabbalah.

The Book Bahir

The Book Bahir is a brief treatise; its modern editions present it as consisting of 130 to 200 paragraphs. It is written in the form of a classical midrashic collection, many paragraphs beginning with the name of a talmudic sage who said it. All paragraphs expound a biblical verse or several verses. The sages to whom the sections are attributed are known *tanaim*, second-century rabbis, but some have fictional names, such as Rabbi Amora. The first paragraph is attributed to Rabbi Nehunia ben ha-Kanah, who is a prominent figure in some treatises of the ancient descenders to the chariot. Because of this, the whole work is often attributed to Rabbi Nehunia. The paragraphs are only loosely connected to each other, and the work does not seem to have a coherent, systematic structure. Many sentences and sections are very difficult to understand, and in some cases there seems to be deliberate mystification, intended to astound the reader. The work begins with a few statements concerning the creation. In the first part of the book there are many discussions of the letters of the alphabet, their shapes, and the meaning of their names. The best-known part of it, the last

third of the work, is an enigmatic description of ten divine powers, which together represent the divine realms.

The author of the book made use of numerous sources that
are known to us, mainly talmudic and midrashic statements
concerning biblical verses, some passages from the Hekhalot
and Merkavah literature, and comments on phrases from traditional prayers. Scores of paragraphs expound sentences and
terms from the ancient Sefer Yezira (The Book of Creation),
which undoubtedly served as a major source of inspiration and
terminology. The author made use of ancient midrashic works
on the letters of the alphabet and developed their ideas and
methods in new directions. This work is the first Jewish treatise that presents in a positive manner the concept of transmi-
gration of souls, the reincarnation or rebirth of the same souls
again and again. The author used several dozens of parables,
presented in a manner found often in classical midrashic literature; most of them begin with the sentence "This is like a human king." when the subject of the parable is God. He also
made use of some medieval sources, such as the writings of Rabbi
Abraham bar Hijja and Rabbi Abraham ibn Ezra, Jewish philosophers of the twelfth century; these references make it possible to fix the time of its writing in the last decades of the
twelfth century, probably about 1185.

The designation of this treatise as the earliest work of the
kabbalah is based on its presentation of three major concepts
that are not found in any earlier Jewish source. The first is the
description of the divine world as consisting of ten hypostases,
ten divine powers, which are called *ma'amarot* (utterances),
which were known in later kabbalistic writings as the ten *sefirot*.
The second is the identification of one of the ten divine powers
as feminine, separate from the other nine, and thus introducing gender dualism into the image of the divine realms. The
third is the description of the divine world as a tree (*ilan*); the
work states that the divine powers are positioned one above
the other like the branches of a tree. It seems that the image
was one of an upside-down tree, its roots above and its branches

growing downward, toward the earth. These three conceptions became characteristic of the kabbalah as a whole (with a few exceptions, including Abraham Abulafia who rejected the concept of the ten *sefirot*), and their presence identifies works as belonging to the kabbalah. In addition to these three concepts there is in the Book Bahir a more dramatic description of the realm of evil than those usually found in earlier Jewish sources, but there is no final separation between God and Satan. The powers of evil are described as the fingers of God's left hand. The dualism of good and evil is found in the kabbalah only three generations later, in the treatise of Rabbi Isaac ha-Cohen of Castile, written about 1265.

The Problem of Gnosticism

Gershom Scholem identified these ideas, found for the first time in the Book Bahir, as gnostic in nature. He believed that the author received them from earlier sources, which, according to him, could be either external, probably Christian gnostics, or from ancient Jewish gnostic tradition secretly transmitted from generation to generation. Scholem described the whole treatise as an anthology, assembled in the late twelfth century, but including several layers of sources going back many centuries. Scholars in the last half-century have intensely debated the origins of the ideas in the Book Bahir, and despite many efforts no source has been identified, neither within Jewish tradition nor outside of it. It seems that a prudent, methodological approach demands that we assume that these ideas are original to the Bahir, developed by its author, until we have proof of an earlier source.

In the middle of the twentieth century—at the time that Scholem and others categorized the Book Bahir, and to some extent the kabbalah in general as including central gnostic characteristics—Gnosticism acquired the dimensions of a world religion, parallel in impact and significance to those of Judaism and Christianity. One of the most forceful expressions of this view was the great monograph on the subject written by Scholem's friend Hans Jonas, which was translated, in an abbreviated form, from German into English as *The Gnostic Religion* (1958). This was the culmination of a long historical-theological development in German thought, best expressed by the views of the German Protestant scholar and theologian Rudolph Bultmann, who considered that Gnosticism included the roots of Christianity. In 1945, when a library of ancient theological works in Coptic was discovered in Nag Hamadi in Egypt, it was interpreted as being a library of ancient gnostic texts, and seemed to validate Bultmann's and Jonas's descriptions of the religion.

Thus, twentieth-century scholarship transformed Gnosticism from a common term that described heretical Christian sects, as presented by the church fathers in the second century CE and later, into a vast religion that served as a source for many Christian and Jewish spiritual phenomena and several medieval heretical movements, includinge the Cathars in Southern France. Many scholars in this field attributed the origins of Gnosticism to ancient Judaism, insisting that there was an ancient, pre-Christian Jewish Gnosticism. Scholem's attitude was greatly influenced by these concepts. He designated the Hekhalot literature as Jewish Gnosticism in a book on the subject published in 1960, and he connected the Book Bahir to this realm. Other scholars tried to establish connections between the early kabbalah and the Christian Chatharic movement in Southern France.

These concepts no longer seem valid. Recent scholarly work on ancient Gnosticism—including that of Michael Williams, Karen King, and Elaine Pagels—denies the existence of such a "third religion." These scholars describe the sects so designated as an expression of the variety and complexity of early Christianity, and reject the anachronistic castigation of "heresy" when discussing them. It seems today that the image of Gnosticism that was prominent in the mid-twentieth century is more an expression of the prejudices and speculations of modern scholars than a reflection of historical reality. The Nag Hamadi library includes treatises concerning many directions and emphases of Christian thought in the early centuries, rather than the expression of one religious worldview. No historical connection has been demonstrated between the ancient gnostic sects and medieval spiritual movements.

A negative can never be proven, yet after a century and a half of searching for Jewish Gnosticism it has to be stated that no evidence of the existence of such a phenomenon has been found. The only basis for speculation in this direction has been the existence of a gnostic religion in the Christian context in ancient times and the Middle Ages; when doubts are cast concerning the existence of pre-Christian and Christian Gnosticism, there is no reason to use this term concerning Jewish phenomena. The assumption that the Book Bahir was influenced either by ancient Jewish gnostic traditions or by Christian Gnosticism, ancient or medieval (that is, Catharic), has not been proven by any textual or terminological evidence. As far as we know today, the mythical concepts that make the Book Bahir a new, radical phenomenon in Jewish spirituality were originated by the author of that book. If so, the kabbalah has to be seen as an innovative Jewish spiritual phenomenon originating in the High Middle Ages. Some of its ideas may be similar to those of other groups within Judaism or outside of it, but no historical connection to other schools has been discovered so far.

3

The Kabbalah
in the Middle Ages

The first kabbalistic text with a known author that reached us is a brief treatise, a commentary on the Sefer Yezira written by Rabbi Isaac ben Abraham the Blind, in Provence near the turn of the thirteenth century. Rabbi Isaac was the son of a great halakhist, Rabbi Abraham of Posquierre, who wrote the first critique of Maimonides's Code of Law. Rabbi Isaac was the teacher and central figure in a small group of kabbalists in Provence, and his teachings were frequently quoted by kabbalists in the next generations. The Provence school developed the concept of the ten *sefirot* in a profound manner, yet they used a terminology that is meaningfully different from that of the Book Bahir. Their worldview was very close to that which is presented in the Book Bahir, but the differences between them prevent us from determining whether they knew the text of the Bahir or whether they developed their system independently. They were familiar with the terminology of Jewish philosophical rationalism of that time, yet they used these concepts in a unique manner, as representing realms and processes within the Godhead.

Rabbi Isaac the Blind was accepted as guide and teacher by a group of kabbalists that was established in the small Catalonian town of Girona, near Barcelona, in the first half of the thirteenth century. The dominant figure in this group was Rabbi

3   After much speculation, today it is widely agreed that the greatest work of the medieval kabbalah, the book Zohar, the Book of Splendor, was written mainly by Rabbi Moshe de Leon in the late 13th century.

Moses ben Nachman (known as Nachmanides), who was regarded as the leader of the Jews in northern Spain. He was a
great halakhist and preacher, and represented Judaism in po-
lemical confrontations with Christian theologians. His main
work is a commentary on the Pentateuch, in which he sometimes hinted at the kabbalistic stratum of the meaning to the
scriptures. The founders of the Girona school were Rabbi Ezra
and Rabbi Azriel, who wrote kabbalistic treatises and commentaries on biblical and talmudic texts. In this circle, the teachings of the Book Bahir and those of the Provence kabbalists
were united into a coherent system, which served as the basis
of medieval kabbalah as a whole. Some writers from this group
participated in the great controversy concerning the philosophy of Maimonides, which erupted in 1232 and continued for
three generations. Some historians of Jewish medieval culture
described the kabbalah as a spiritual reaction to Jewish rationalism, presenting a more experiential religiosity against the
"cold, distant" conceptions of the rationalists. The Girona
kabbalists were versed in the teachings of Jewish philosophy,
but they integrated them, like the Provence kabbalists, within
their nonrationalistic system. The great contribution of the
Girona writers to the history of the kabbalah was their presentation of the ancient religious texts, the Bible and the Talmud,
as including a hidden kabbalistic stratum of meaning, that can
be understood only by scholars versed in the secrets of the
kabbalistic tradition. They tended not to reveal these secrets in
their popular works, and wrote several traditional treatises on
ethics (especially on repentance), in which they presented themselves as following talmudic teachings without presenting their
underlying kabbalistic worldview.

In the second half of the thirteenth century, several kabbalistic circles were active in Spain. Among them were those of
the brothers Rabbi Jacob and Rabbi Isaac, sons of Rabbi Jacob
ha-Cohen of Castile, and that of the lonely mystic wanderer
Rabbi Abraham Abulafia, who developed a different direction
of kabbalistic speculation. Abulafia's numerous treatises have

4 Permutations of divine names and names of angels in a protective amulet.

been described by Scholem as "ecstatic" or "prophetic" kabbalah, which emphasized the visionary and experiential aspect, and relied on novel approaches to the Hebrew alphabet and the numbers as the source of divine truths. Abulafia's teachings represented the mystical tendencies among kabbalists, instead of the theosophical and traditional speculations that prevailed in other circles.

One of his disciples was Rabbi Joseph Gikatilla, who later changed his mind and joined the school of Rabbi Moses de Leon, the author of the Zohar. Gikatilla wrote one of the most influential presentations of the kabbalistic worldview, *Shaaey Ora* (The Gates of Light), a summary of the teachings of the kabbalah arranged according to the order of the ten *sefirot*. Another circle of kabbalists assembled around Rabbi Shlomo ben Adrat, known by the acronym RaSHBAh, a great halakhist and leader at the end of the thirteenth and the beginning of the fourteenth centuries. This period can be regarded as the peak of the creativity and influence of the medieval kabbalah, which began to spread to Italy, Germany, and the east, and became a meaningful, though still esoteric and marginal, component of Jewish religious culture. The most important circle was that which assembled around Rabbi Moses de Leon in northern Spain, the circle that produced the greatest work of the medieval kabbalah, the book Zohar.

The Zohar

The belief in the book Zohar as a traditional work standing beside the Bible and the Talmud as the three pillars of Jewish faith and ancient tradition has become an article of faith in modern orthodox Judaism. Confidence that the Zohar was actually written by the sage Rabbi Shimeon bar Yohai in the early second century CE defines a Jew as completely orthodox, and doubting this is regarded as the beginning of heresy and denial of Jewish tradition. It became an article of faith for the Christian kabbalah as well. The fact is that since the end of the fifteenth century there were Jewish thinkers who doubted this attribution and stated that the work is a medieval one, written by Rabbi Moses de Leon, who died in 1305. Rabbi Judah Arieh of Modena presented a detailed, systematic argument to that effect in the middle in the seventeenth century. Among modern scholars there were some who were hesitant, but Heinrich Graetz, the great nineteenth-century historian, accepted and developed Modena's argument and Gershom Scholem presented a detailed justification for the medieval origin in his *Major Trends in Jewish Mysticism* (1941). Scholem's closest disciple, Isaiah Tishby, further developed this line of reasoning in his *Wisdom of the Zohar* (Hebrew, 1949; English, 1989) and several other studies. Today, while there is still some debate concerning the exact date of the Zohar's composition and concerning the participation of some other kabbalists in the writing of the work, there seems to be no doubt that the Zohar was written mainly by Rabbi Moses de Leon in the last decades of the thirteenth century.

De Leon, who wrote several kabbalistic works other than the Zohar, used to sell portions of the Zohar to people interested in esoteric traditions, claiming that he was copying it from an ancient manuscript that reached him from the Holy Land. We have an incomplete document written by a kabbalist a short time after de Leon's death, in which a story is told about the authorship of the Zohar. According to it, de Leon left his widow and daughter destitute when he died. A rich kabbalist offered them a large sum of money if they would sell him the original manuscript from which de Leon claimed to have copied the various portions of the Zohar. The widow said that she was unable to do that, because her late husband "wrote from his own mind" and there was no source from which he was copying. Scholars have made different interpretations of this document, and clearly it cannot alone serve as proof. Yet, integrated with numerous philological and linguistic characteristics, it seems that De Leon was the principal author of the main part of the Zohar. The Zohar is actually a library, comprised of more than a score of treatises. The main part, the body of the Zohar, is a homiletical commentary in Aramaic on all the portions of the five books of the Pentateuch, as if they were ancient midrashic works (though they were not, as a rule, written in Aramaic). Among the other treatises included in the body of the Zohar are: the Midrash ha-Neelam (The Esoteric Midrash), written partly in Hebrew, and probably the first part of this huge work to be written; a section dedicated to the discussion of the commandments; and others including revelations by a wondrous old man (*sava*) and a boy (*yenuka*). The most esoteric discussions, regarded as the holiest part of the Zohar, are called Idra Rabba (The Large Assembly) and Idra Zuta (The Small Assembly). A later writer imitating the style and language of de Leon added two works to the Zohar in the beginning of the fourteenth century: Raaya Mehemna (The Faithful Shepherd, meaning Moses), which is presented in several sections of the work, and Tikuney Zohar (Emendations of the Zohar), which was printed as an independent work. A fifth volume in the Zohar library is the Zohar Hadash (The New Zohar), a collection of material from manuscripts that were not included in the first edition of the Zohar. The body of the Zohar was first printed in Mantua in 1558–1560 in three volumes, and this is the traditional edition that was printed many times since. Another edition was published in Cremona, Italy, in 1559 in one large volume. Rav Yehuda Ashlag published a translation of the whole Zohar into Hebrew with a comprehensive traditional commentary in many volumes in the middle of the twentieth century. The English reader can profit from the large anthology of Zohar sections in Tishby's *Wisdom of the Zohar* and Daniel Matt's translation and commentary (first two volumes, 2004).

The teachings of the Zohar are presented within a framework of a sophisticated literary structure. It is a narrative of the experiences and spiritual adventures of a group of sages whose leaders are Rabbi Shimeon bar Yohai and his son, Rabbi Eleazar. The other members are also early second-century sages. The literary framework was inspired by many stories scattered in talmudic and midrashic literature, which are integrated into a structured narrative that serves as a background for the sermons and the events described in the work. The Zohar is thus a pseudo-epigraphical work, which is not only attributed to an ancient sage but also creates an elaborate fictional narrative that supports most of the sermons included in it. The narrative includes descriptions of the group's wanderings from place to place in the Holy Land, the sages' meetings with wondrous celestial persons who reveal great secrets, and their visions of occurrences in the divine realm. The sections called "assemblies" (idrot) were probably modeled after a description of a gathering of mystics in the ancient Hekhalot Rabbati. The narrative includes a biography of Rabbi Shimeon, including a description of his last illness and death. Yet, the message of the Zohar is delivered in the classical, midrashic homiletical fashion, exegesis of verses in the Torah and other parts of scriptures in the elaborate hermeneutical methodology perfected by the ancient sermonists of the midrash. Many of the Zohar's sermons are presented in a sophisticated, elegant way, making it one of the peaks of Jewish literary creativity in the Middle Ages.

The author of the Zohar put on, when writing this work, several layers of disguise, hiding his own personality, time, and language. He created an artificial language, an Aramaic that is not found in the same way anywhere else, innovating a vocabulary and grammatical forms. He attributed the work to ancient sages, and created a narrative that occurs in a distant place at another time. These disguises allowed him a freedom from contemporary restrictions. This is evident when the Zohar is compared to the Hebrew kabbalistic works of Rabbi Moses de Leon. Often there are similar, or almost identical, paragraphs in the Zohar and the Hebrew works, yet the Zohar differs in the richness, dynamism, and boldness of its metaphors, which are not found in the Hebrew texts. The radical mythological descriptions of the divine powers, the unhesitating use of detailed erotic language, and the visionary character of many sections—these are unequaled in Jewish literature, and place the Zohar among the most daring and radical works of religious literature and mysticism in any language. The paradox is that despite these radical elements Jewish readers could treat the Zohar as a conventional midrash. The use of traditional sages and old homiletical methodologies allowed the Zohar to be accepted as a traditional, authoritative work of Jewish religiosity.

This huge library includes every imaginable subject, yet at its center are two interwoven themes. The first theme includes "the secret of genesis" and "the secret of the *merkavah*," that is, the detailed description of the emergence of the *sefirot* from the eternal, perfect, hidden divine realm and the emanation of the divine system that created and governs the world. This is a dynamic myth, unifying theogony, cosmogony, and cosmology into one whole myth. The second is the unification of this speculation concerning the divine world with traditional Jewish rituals, commandments, and ethical norms. Jewish religious practice was elaborately and meticulously connected with the characteristics and dynamic processes in the realm of the *sefirot* and the struggle against the *sitra ahra*, the powers of evil. In this way, the Zoharic worldview is based on the concept of reflection: everything is the reflection of everything else. The verses of scriptures reflect the emanation and structure of the divine world; as does the human body, in the anthropomorphic conception of the *sefirot*, and the human soul, which originates from the divine realm and in its various parts reflects the functions and dynamism of the *sefirot*. The universe reflects in its structure the divine realms, and events in it, in the past and in the present, parallel the mythological processes of the divine powers. The various sermons of the Zohar present these and other parallels in great detail. The structure of the temple in Jerusalem and the ancient rituals practiced in it are a reflection of all other processes, in the universe, in man, and within the heavenly realms. Historical events, the phases of human life, the rituals of the Jewish Sabbath, and the festivals are all integrated into this vast picture. Everything is a metaphor for everything else. In many sections the ultimate redemption, the messianic era, is included within these descriptions. All this is presented as a secret message, a heavenly revelation to ancient sages, using conventional, authoritative methodologies.

The Kabbalah in the Fourteenth and Fifteenth Centuries

The influence of the Zohar spread slowly in the fourteenth and fifteenth centuries, but gradually its worldview came to dominate the scattered circles of kabbalists in Europe, North Africa, and the Middle East. However, the peak of creativity that was reached during the period in which the Zohar was composed was not maintained. The last generations of the Middle Ages saw the kabbalah spread in several rather isolated circles throughout the Jewish world, and only a handful of great kabbalistic works have reached us from this period. Some were written by well-known scholars, such as Joseph ben Shalom Ashkenazi, whose *Commentary on the Work of Genesis* and other work had meaningful influence. Others were pseudo-epigraphic, imitating to some extent the format of the Zohar, including the Sefer ha-Kanah, a commentary on the commandments attributed to the tradition of the ancient sage Rabbi Nehunia ben ha-Kanah, and Sefer ha-Peliah, probably by the same author, which includes an anthology of older kabbalistic texts. In Italy, the tradition of kabbalistic speculations that was started by Rabbi Menahem Recanatti was continued, and in central Europe many treatises that integrated the Spanish kabbalah with the traditions of the Hasidey Ashkenaz exerted meaningful influence. Rabbi Menahem Zioni's commentary on the Torah and his treatise on the powers of evil represented Ashkenazi creativity in this field.

The messianic element in the kabbalah, presented by Rabbi Isaac ha-Cohen of Castile and developed in the Zohar, became prominent in the writings of kabbalists in Spain and elsewhere in the middle and second half of the fifteenth century. The increasing persecutions of Spanish Jewry in that century, culminating in the exile of the Jews from Spain in 1492, changed the spiritual atmosphere in the Jewish communities and caused the decline of the hitherto-dominant rationalistic philosophy and increased interest in the kabbalah. The sense of exile became central in the consciousness of Jewish intellectuals, and messianic speculations held an increasing place in Jewish religious culture. Several kabbalistic circles developed in this period of intense apocalyptic and messianic inclinations. One of the leaders, the Spanish kabbalist Rabbi Joseph dela Reina, became the hero of a well-known story, which described an attempt to overcome the Satanic powers and bring forth redemption by using kabbalistic and magical means. Another kabbalist, Rabbi Abraham berabi Eliezer ha-Levi, wrote a series of kabbalistic-apocalyptic treatises; he continued writing after the exile from Spain, when he settled in Jerusalem. This was the beginning of the process that, in the sixteenth century, transformed the kabbalah from the realm of scattered esoteric circles to the dominant spiritual doctrine of the Jewish people in early modern times.

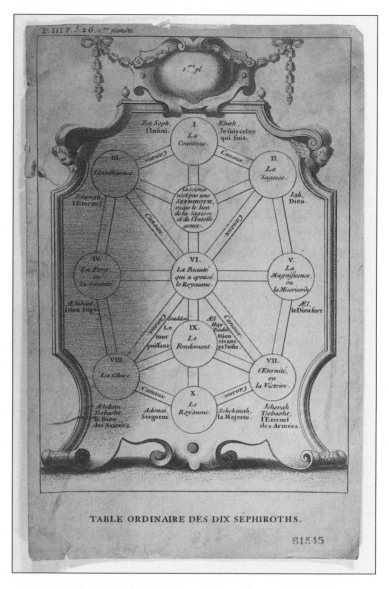

5   A Latin schematic drawing of the ten divine emanations, the *sefirot*, which together represent the power of God.

4

Main Ideas of the Medieval Kabbalah

The kabbalah in the Middle Ages inherited from ancient Jewish traditions a prohibition on discussing matters that relate to the divine world (*ma'aseh merkavah*), as well as a sizable body of descriptions and speculations concerning the nature and structure of that same realm. The result of this clash between the kabbalah's interest in describing the divine world and the ancient ban was three-fold: first, the medieval kabbalists insisted on esotericism, keeping the kabbalah secret; second, they used pseudo-epigraphy, attributing their works to ancient figures, mainly *tanaim*, the sages of the Mishnah; and, third, they were traditionalists, who claimed that they were not revealing anything new, just copying or writing down traditions received from previous generations, either orally or in secret writings. An additional precaution used by several kabbalistic writers was obscurantism and mystification, using hints and opaque references that cannot be understood by any "outside" reader who is not familiar with the particular terminology.

From a historical point of view, the main reason that the early kabbalists were not a focus of controversy and criticism for their radical new ideas was literary conservatism. The kabbalah is a new spiritual phenomenon that differed in a meaningful way from orthodox conceptions and worldviews. Yet, they expressed themselves in the most traditional literary forms, so that to an "outsider" their works looked like orthodox collections of ancient midrashim; or commentaries on biblical books, talmudic treatises, the prayers, or the ancient Sefer Yezira; or works of Jewish ethics (*sifrut musar*); or sermons and homiletic literature. Eight hundred years of intense and dynamic kabbalistic creativity did not produce a genre that can be called "kabbalistic literature." There is no external distinction between kabbalistic homiletic literature and nonkabbalistic works of the same genre. There is no way to determine whether a work employs the kabbalah or not by looking at its form and structure. In this way, with few exceptions, kabbalistic works blended into Jewish literary traditions.

The price the kabbalists had to pay for their successful blending in with traditional Jewish culture was the suppression of any expressions of individual spiritual and mystical experiences. A direct contact with the divine realm was not an acceptable part of Jewish culture in this period; it was regarded as a characteristic of the ancient past, when prophets and other people selected by God were allowed to experience divine revelation. In contemporary (that is, medieval and modern) religious experience God is met through the interpretation of the verses of ancient, scriptural revelation, or during the intense *kavanah* (the spiritual intention added to the traditional prayer texts) in prayer. Jewish culture of this period did not recognize, either theologically or in literary conventions, individual experiences of receiving information and instruction from God. A marginal exception was the practice of "questions from heaven," when some rabbis, mainly in the thirteenth century, indulged in presenting questions of law to God before going to sleep, and then interpreting their dream as a response to them. The kabbalists could not—assuming that they wished to do so— present their experiential spiritual world in direct writing. It is now the role of scholars to try to find traces of visionary and mystical experiences in the homiletic and exegetical writings of the medieval and modern writers. Very few kabbalists revealed in their writings the experiential basis of their speculations; the best known among those who did in the Middle Ages was Abraham Abulafia. In later times, Rabbi Joseph Karo, Rabbi Moshe Hayyim Luzzatto, and others attributed their works to a celestial messenger, a *magid*, who was conceived as a supreme angel or a divine power. Yet these are a few exceptions in the vast kabbalistic literature, which in most cases is dressed in the form of impersonal exegetical and homiletic writing. In some cases, the reader may confidently discern a mystical experience hiding behind a homiletic presentation: some intense, visionary passages in the Zohar, for instance, indicate such experiential subtext rather clearly. Such an investigation, however, is obviously subjective in nature, and observations of this kind can never be proved in a methodological, systematic scholarly manner. In many cases, undoubtedly, Jewish mystics successfully disguised themselves as traditional commentators and preachers, preserving their loyalty to the presentation of the kabbalah as transmitted tradition rather than individual mystical experience.

Ein Sof

The kabbalah's starting point for presenting the structure of the innermost divine realms is surprisingly similar to that of the rationalistic philosophers who were in the center of Jewish theological creativity between the tenth and the fifteenth centuries. The concept of an infinite, perfect supreme being that cannot change, a concept absent from Jewish thought in antiquity, is dominant in both philosophy and kabbalah. This concept, which was expressed in the most powerful terms by Aristotelian thinkers when they discussed the primal cause or the unmoved mover, was accepted wholeheartedly by Jewish medieval thinkers. Kabbalistic terminology often used the term *"ein sof,"* no end, infinite, to designate this supreme entity. Tishby once wrote that the rationalistic philosophers and the kabbalists presented the same questions; only their answers were different. The process of emanation that brought forth the system of the *sefirot* was the kabbalistic answer to the question, "How can anything different emerge from the unchanging and eternal divinity?"

The term *"ein sof"* itself does not carry any particular meaning. It is a negative phrase that could be replaced by any other negative one: "no beginning" or "eternal" could be used in its stead, as well as any other designation of divine infinity. Unlike the appellations of the *sefirot*, the *ein sof* is not represented by any anthropomorphic or ethical phrase. Many kabbalists insisted that the *ein sof* is not indicated by any biblical phrase, because its perfection and unchanging character put it beyond language, even divine language. It seems that the convention to call this entity by the term *"ein sof"* developed from philosophical and poetic series of negatives that were used to denote the Godhead, and *ein sof* was the most common and routine one. The realm of *ein sof* in the kabbalah is therefore beyond language, beyond any kind of description, and essentially it is not different from the rationalistic designations of the infinite supreme eternal entity. Some kabbalists, however, did include the *ein sof* in the system of the *sefirot* and identified it, though often in ambiguous terms, with the first *sefirah*, *keter*. This is found even in some sections of the Zohar.

An indication of the problems that the kabbalists faced when trying to reconcile the infinity of *ein sof* with the distinct entities the *sefirot* is found in a variety of systems that postulated the existence of "roots" of the *sefirot* within the *ein sof* itself. One formulation of this kind is the concept of the *zahzahot*, which described three kinds of supreme, pure sources of light existing within the *ein sof*, which were the source of the emanation of the *sefirot*. This and other such systems attempt to build a bridge between the timelessness of the *ein sof* and the *sefirot*, which exist in time. In other presentations the ten *sefirot* have an early, pure, potential image within the infinity of *ein sof*. The most important aspect of *ein sof* in kabbalistic thought is as the ultimate source of the flow of the purest divine light (*shefa*) that constantly provides the power to exist in both divine and earthly realms. Emanation is not a one-time event, but an on-going vital process that maintains the existence of all beings. There is a close similarity between these kabbalistic concepts and the teachings of various neo-Platonic schools in the Middle Ages, and the centrality of the process of emanation in the kabbalistic descriptions of divinity attest to this close relationship. The kabbalists differed from the neo-Platonists in the intense dynamism and mythological elements that they introduced into their system, especially in the lower realms of existence, and in their belief in the capacity of human deeds and behavior to influence processes in the divine world.

Sefirot

When kabbalists use a term such as the *"shekhinah"* for the feminine aspect in the divine world, their writings tend to blend together with traditional Jewish culture as a whole, because this term is prominent in Jewish texts in many forms and meanings, so that it cannot be used as a distinguishing characteristic separating kabbalah from nonkabbalah. The term *"sefirot,"* the ten divine powers that comprise the divine realm, and the many other terms that accompany it, however, is regarded as a particularly kabbalistic one. It often serves as the most obvious term that marks the text as a kabbalistic one. This is not a foolproof observation. There were kabbalists who deliberately opposed this term and everything that it represented, including Abraham Abulafia in the second half of the thirteenth century. There were kabbalists, such as Rabbi Moshe Hayyim Luzzatto in the beginning of the eighteenth century, who tried to hide their distinctive worldview by avoiding this term, though they conveyed the content in other ways. Some Hasidic writers, and some modern religious thinkers, deliberately avoided the use of distinctive kabbalistic terminology. But bearing these exceptions in mind, in most cases the use of the term *"sefirot"* is the clearest indication of a kabbalistic worldview and of a text's reliance on kabbalistic traditions and sources. A statement that "a work which employs the concept of the ten *sefirot* using this or parallel terms is a kabbalistic one" is not accurate, but it may be as close as one can get to a definition of a kabbalistic work.

The most important exception to this rule is the work in which the term was coined and used—the ancient Sefer Yezira (The Book of Creation), which used this term to denote several characteristics of the cosmos. It is an original concept in the Sefer Yezira. However, the kabbalists in the late twelfth century and the thirteenth gave it a completely new meaning. In early kabbalistic works this term is not the dominant one. The Book Bahir, for instance, despite its comprehensive reliance on the Sefer Yezira, did not use the term for the powers in the divine world; it preferred the term "*midot*" (characteristic, qualities) and "*ma'amarot*" (utterances). The Zohar also did not use it frequently, employing instead many other terms. But most kabbalistic works did use the term "*sefirot*," and this conception of God is the most prominent characteristic of kabbalistic tradition.

The question "What are the *sefirot*?" is one that cannot be answered, because every kabbalist has his own individual conceptions and emphases on this subject. This is the core of envisioning and understanding the divine world, and therefore the most meaningful differences between kabbalists are expressed in their presentations of this realm. Any generalization in this context is necessarily misleading. Many hundreds of kabbalistic writings—intense mythical descriptions on one hand and precise, pseudological presentations on the other—used identical or similar terminology to express radically different worldviews. Meaningful differences can be found even within the same works, including the Zohar itself. The following presentation of the *sefirot* necessarily overlooks the individual and creative contributions of the kabbalists. It is like describing the structure of a sonnet without discussing the different contents of each poem. It gives the illusion that the kabbalah is a doctrine that can be studied, marginalizing the most important, individual characteristics. Bearing these reservations in mind, some bold outlines can be drawn.

One of the most common, and most meaningful, descriptions of the system of the *sefirot* is the anthropomorphic one. The three upper *sefirot* represent the divine head, the next two are the right and left arms, the sixth is the body or the heart, which also represents the masculinity of this figure. The next two represent the legs; the ninth, the phallus; and the tenth represents a separate body, that of the female divine power. This image is based on the ancient mystical text the Shiur Komah in which the divine body of the creator is described, accompanied by secret names and measurements for each limb (following the description of the beloved in Songs 5:10–16). Thus portrayed, the divine realm is conceived in mythical, dynamic terms, tending to emphasize processes that are expressed in erotic terms. The image of the *sefirot* as a gigantic anthropomorphic figure is a central one in many kabbalistic works, including the Zohar, while other kabbalists tended to marginalize these terms and use more "logical" ones.

Another most prominent system found in most kabbalistic works is that of the *sefirot* representing the stages of divine emanation. Within the supreme, perfect, and infinite Godhead, the *ein sof,* a point began shining, expressing the divine will to create something beside itself (*keter*). This will was transformed into a plan, a program for the future—this is divine wisdom (*hokhmah*). The third sefirah, *binah*, is portrayed in this system as the supreme fountain from which divine existence emerges; the will and the wisdom, which are just potentialities, are transformed here into actual emanated entities. The first two powers to emerge from *binah* are the modes by which existence is regulated: the right side, *hesed*, expressing love and mercy, and the left, *din* or *gevurah*, representing divine strict law and justice. They are united in the sixth sefirah, *tiferet*, creating a mixture that sustains an existence that cannot suffer just pure love or just pure justice. *Nezah* and *hod* represent lower forms of *hesed* and *din*, and the ninth, *yesod*, is the vehicle by which divine power is poured into the lower realms. The tenth, the feminine power, is the intermediary that transfers the divine flow to creation, and it is the power of divine revelation to creatures. The system of the *sefirot* is thus conceived as a demiurgic entity, a kind of detailed logos, which bridges the abstract, infinite Godhead and the functions needed to emanate the divine powers, endows them with their specific functions, and enables them to sustain and provide for all existence.

Most kabbalists integrated the biblical names of God into the system of the *sefirot*. Thus, for instance, the tetragrammaton—the biblical name of God written in four letters, YHVH, which, in Hebrew, it is forbidden to pronounce—was interpreted as presenting the first *sefirah*, *keter*, in the almost-hidden little point above the first letter, yod, which represents the second *sefirah*, divine wisdom (*hokhmah*). The first letter, he, is the binah, followed by the vav, which represents the number six, and thus relates to the six central *sefirot* from *hesed* to *yesod*. The last he represents the female entity, the *shekhinah*. This just one of the many interpretations of this name, and all other divine appellations in the Bible and Talmud are conceived as representing one or a group of *sefirot*. It can be stated that the system of the *sefirot* is viewed by most kabbalists to represent hidden, secret name or names of God. In this way, the myth of the ten entities and the linguistic expressions of the divine realm are united in the kabbalistic worldview. Kabbalists utilized the names that were used by prekabbalistic esoterics, including the names of twelve, forty-two, and seventy-two letters, and integrated them in this system.

The kabbalists translated almost all the classical—biblical and talmudic—terms into their system of divine emanations. Every linguistic "pair" has been interpreted as relating to the gender duality in the divine world, the masculine and the feminine: the sun and the moon, heaven and earth, and day and night were understood to represent this duality. The heroes of biblical narratives were identified with these supreme emanations; Abraham, Isaac, and Jacob are *hesed*, *din*, and *tiferet*; Joseph is *yesod*; David is the *shekhinah*; and many other combinations. The structure of the human soul was conceived as reflecting this structure, the various powers in the human psyche being identified with the divine powers. In the medieval kabbalah we find systems in which the realm of the *sefirot* is duplicated, multiplied, and repeated, so that the number of *sefirot* may range from twenty to one hundred. In Lurianic kabbalah the number of the *sefirot* is infinite, because every entity—material or spiritual, high and low—is described as being comprised of different combinations of this system. The *sefirot* cease to be individual entities and become the basic structure of everything.

Various kabbalists described the *sefirot* as personifications of ethical values that are combined by God in order to govern the world by them. Others emphasized the philosophical, pseudorational character of the system, presenting it as an almost neo-Platonic series of divine emanations. Others divided them or duplicated them into "worlds," various layers of existence descending from pure divinity to more material, physical realms. Most kabbalists presented intricate combinations of these *serifot* and other elements.

The *Shekhinah*

The feminine power in the divine world, best known by the name *shekhinah* (divine residence) is one of the most prominent concepts that distinguishes the kabbalah from other Jewish worldviews, and it had a significant impact in shaping the kabbalistic theory and practice. In kabbalistic literature she is designated by many scores, if not hundreds, of names and titles, and numerous biblical verses have been interpreted as relating to her. The employs of the *shekhinah* are described in great detail in the Zohar, and coming into spiritual contact with her is a main component of kabbalistic rituals. She is the tenth and lowest power in the divine realm, and therefore closest to the material, created world and to human beings. She is the divine power that is envisioned by the prophets, and after their death the righteous reside in her realm. As the lowest *sefirah* she is closest to the sufferings of the people of Israel, and is most exposed to the machinations of the evil powers, who constantly try to establish dominion over her. Being feminine, she is the weakest among the divine powers, and the satanic forces can achieve a hold and draw her away from her husband (the male divine figure, often the totality of the other nine *sefirot*, or, sometimes specifically the sixth *sefirah*, *tiferet)*, thus disrupting the harmony of the divine world. She is dependent on divine light, which flows from above; she is like the moon, which does not have light of its own, only the reflection of the sun's light. The redemption of the *shekhinah* from her exile and suffering and reuniting her with her husband is the main purpose of many kabbalistic rituals.

Unlike many other phenomena that characterize the kabbalah, the history of the *shekhinah* is rather well known. Scholars agree about the development of this concept, although they have different views about the source of its conception as a feminine power. The term *"shekhinah"* is not found in the Bible, and it was formulated in talmudic literature from the biblical verb designating the residence (*shkn*) of God in the temple in Jerusalem and among the Jewish people. *"Shekhinah"* is used in rabbinic literature as one of the many abstract titles or references to God, which replaced in their language the proper names of God used in the Bible. Like "the Holy one Blessed Be He" (*ha-kadosh baruch hu*), "heaven" (*shamayim*), "the name" (*ha-shem*), "the place" (*ha-makom*), and others, it has been used to designate God without naming him, and the terms are interchangeable. Indeed, there are talmudic-midrashic statements that in one place use *shekhinah* and, in another, one of the similar phrases. It did retain some particular flavor of the divine power residing within Jerusalem and the people of Israel, but was always one of the synonyms used to designate God. Though the word *"shekhinah"* in Hebrew is grammatically a feminine one, there is no indication in ancient literature of any particular feminine characteristics that separate the *shekhinah* from other appellations of God.

A change occurred in the early centuries of the Middle Ages. Some late midrashic compilations use the term *"shekhinah"* to designate an entity that is separate from God himself. Rav Saadia Gaon, the great leader of the Jews in Babylonia, made a clear, theological statement to this effect in the first half of the tenth century. In his philosophical work, "Beliefs and Ideas," written in Arabic around 930 CE, which is the first comprehensive, systematic Jewish rationalistic theology, he used the term *"shekhinah"* to overcome the difficult problem of the anthropomorphic descriptions of God in scriptures. As a rationalist, Saadia could not accept physical references to the infinite, perfect God, so he postulated that all such references relate not to God himself but to a created angel, supreme and brilliant but still a creature, which is called *kavod* (glory, honor) in the Bible and *shekhinah* by the rabbis. Since Saadia, therefore, the *shekhinah* is conceived in Jewish writings as a lower power, separate from God, which has its main function in the process of revelation to the prophets. It can assume physical characteristics, and it can be envisioned by human eyes.

The next stage in the development of the concept of the *shekhinah* occurred in the works of eleventh- and twelfth-century commentators, philosophers, and theologians, who were reluctant to accept that the descriptions of God by the ancient prophets are actually references to a created angel. Several of them, the most prominent was Rabbi Abraham ibn Ezra in the middle of the twelfth century, described the *kavod-shekhinah* as an emanated divine power, which can assume characteristics that allow revelation and anthropomorphic descriptions. This concept was used by the esoterics and pietists of the Rhineland and other writers. By the late twelfth century the *shekhinah* was conceived as a separate, emanated divine power that is revealed to the prophets and assumes other worldly functions. In all these sources there is no hint of this entity being feminine.

The Book Bahir, the first work of the kabbalah, is the earliest source we have that might imagine the *shekhinah* as a feminine power. The author used ibn Ezra's concepts of the identity of the *shekhinah* and the *kavod* as a separate, emanated power, but in several sections, especially in the context of parables, he refers to this power in feminine terms. She is described as wife, bride, and daughter of the masculine power. There is very little in the Bahir in this context that is clearly erotic, but subsequent kabbalists understood its sometimes cryptic references as indicating the presence of a feminine divine power in the realm of the *sefirot*. Thirteenth-century kabbalists in Gerona and Castile, as well as Abraham Abulafia, accepted this image, though they developed it in a minimal, restrained manner. The Zohar, and other kabbalistic works from the end of the thirteenth century and the beginning of the fourteenth, made the myth of the feminine *shekhinah* a central element in their descriptions of the divine world, made her the purpose of rituals and religious experiences, and established this as one of the most prominent components of the kabbalistic worldview.

Gershom Scholem regarded the concept of the feminine *shekhinah* in the Book Bahir as the appearance of a gnostic concept within the early kabbalah. It could be regarded as an ancient Jewish gnostic concept that surfaced in the kabbalah in the Middle Ages after being transmitted in secret for many centuries, or the result of the influence of Christian Gnosticism, which emphasized the role of feminine powers in the divine world. Many scholars accepted Scholem's explanation, and saw the image of an androgynous, gender-dualistic divine world as the result of gnostic impact. Recently, however, several scholars have presented a different approach: The femininity of the *shekhinah* is the result of the influence of the intense Christian worship of the Madonna, the Mother of Christ, that peaked in the twelfth century. This occurred, according to them, in Provence or northern Spain in the late twelfth century, and therefore it does not indicate an ancient Jewish gnostic concept. This explanation may reflect the recent decline in the belief that there was a gnostic "third religion" that greatly influenced both Judaism and Christianity. There is no definite proof of that or any detail or phrase that indicates the impact of the Christian concept of the Virgin Mary on early kabbalistic terminology and ideas.

The third possibility is to assume, in the absence of definite proof to the contrary, that the femininity of the *shekhinah* results from the individual inspiration of the Bahir's author. This can be understood from a literary point of view as the result of his frequent, almost obsessive, use of parables of kings and queens, princes and princesses, as well as a unique mystical experience. From a methodological point of view, it is always better to assume the minimal conclusion attested by the texts until another one can be presented with adequate documentation.

"The Emanations on the Left"

Rabbinic tradition, represented by talmudic-midrashic literature, is remarkably ignorant of the existence of independent powers of evil that struggle against divine goodness and create a dualistic state of affairs in creation. Satan in his various manifestations in this literature is a power within the divine court and God's system of justice. The esoteric and mystical treatises of the ancient period, the Hekhalot and Merkavah literature, did not present an intensified image of the powers of evil. In the apocryphal and pseudo-epigrahical literature of antiquity, as well as in the Dead Sea Scrolls and the literature of early Christianity, we do find some more pronounced tendencies toward dualism of good and evil, but most of these texts were not known to Medieval Jewish thinkers. The first indication of a satanic rebellion against God in rabbinic literature is found in the eighth-century midrash *Pirkey de-Rabbi Eliezer*, but this seemed to have little impact until the twelfth century. The section of this midrash in which the rebellion is described was included in the Book Bahir, serving as its concluding chapter.

The formulation of the powers of evil as an independent enemy of the divine, and the description of human life as being conducted in a dualistic universe in which evil and good are in constant struggle, is the contribution of the kabbalah to Jewish worldview. There are some indications of an intensified conception of evil in the Book Bahir and in the works of the early kabbalists in Provence, but the first kabbalistic dualistic system was presented in a brief treatise written by Rabbi Isaac ben Jacob ha-Cohen, entitled *Treatise on the Emanations on the Left*. This treatise, written in Castile about 1265, describes a parallel system of seven divine evil powers, the first of which is called Samael and the seventh, feminine one is called Lilith. While both of these figures have a long history in Jewish writings before Rabbi Isaac, it seems that he was the first to bring them together and present them as a divine couple, parallel to God and the *shekhinah*, who rule over a diverse structure of evil demons, who struggle for dominion in the universe against the powers of goodness, the emanations on the right. It should be remembered that "left" (*smol*) and Samael are almost homonyms in Hebrew. Rabbi Isaac was the first to present a hierarchy of evil powers and evil phenomena, including illnesses and pestilence, connecting all of them into one system.

Rabbi Isaac presented a mythological description of the relationship between the satanic powers; he described the "older Lilith" and "younger Lilith," the latter being the spouse of Asmodeus, whom Samael covets. The realm of evil includes images of dragons and snakes and other threatening monsters. He claimed to have used various ancient sources and traditions, but it seems that they are fictional ones, invented by him to give an aura of authority to his novel worldview. He used older sources, including the writings of Rabbi Eleazar of Worms, but changed their meaning and inserted his dualistic views into them.

Rabbi Isaac did not assign a religious role to human beings in the process of the struggle against evil. Unlike Rabbi Ezra of Girona, he did not find the root of evil's existence in the events in the Garden of Eden and human sin. Evil evolved from the

6 An amulet designed to repel the power of Lilith.

third *sefirah, binah,* as a distorted side effect of the process of emanation. It continues throughout the history of the world, and will come to an end in the final, apocalyptic struggle between Samael and the messiah. The last pages of this treatise are dedicated to a detailed description of the final battles between angels and demons, and the ultimate triumph of the messiah. Thus, this treatise is the first presentation of a dualistic concept of the cosmos in kabbalistic literature, and at the same time it is the first to describe messianic redemption in terms of the kabbalistic worldview. Earlier kabbalists hardly paid any attention to the subjects of messianism and redemption; only in Rabbi Isaac's treatise do we find the first integration of kabbalah and messianism, a phenomenon that later became central to the kabbalah and a main characteristic of its teachings.

Rabbi Isaac was one of the writers of a school of kabbalists that flourished in Castile in the middle and second half of the thirteenth century. Other writers of this group, including his elder brother, Rabbi Jacob ben Jacob ha-Cohen, did not participate in the development of these dualistic ideas, nor do we find in any of their works a trace of the messianic apocalypse presented by Rabbi Isaac. Only one of his disciples, Rabbi Moshe of Burgos, wrote a treatise that follows the worldview of the *Emanations on the Left.* All other kabbalists completely ignored it, with one most meaningful exception. Rabbi Moses de Leon, the author of the Zohar, accepted Rabbi Isaac's mythology and put it at the center of the teachings of the Zohar. Rabbi Isaac's works were almost completely forgotten in the history of kabbalistic literature, and only a handful of later writers were familiar with them, until they were published by Gershom Scholem in the 1920s and 1930s. Yet, his worldview became one of the most important images and ideas of the kabbalah as a whole, after it was included and developed in the sermons of the Zohar, and was, therefore, regarded as a traditional foundation of the kabbalah. De Leon even preserved a hint to the title of Rabbi Isaac's treatise. In the Zohar the realm of evil is called *sitra ahra*, an Aramaic phrase meaning "the other side." "Other" is the unmentionable left side, which is also the name of God's archenemy, Samael.

Kabbalah and Spiritualization

Judaism entered the High Middle Ages in Europe in a disadvantageous position compared to the two other scriptural religions that dominated the medieval world. Christianity and Islam preceded it in adopting and accommodating their spiritual world to the teachings of Greek philosophy. The concept of God as infinite and purely spiritual demanded that religious life emphasize the spiritual aspects rather than the practical and material ones. The concept that God is absolutely perfect and eternal denied any possibility of interaction between God and the world. The ancient Platonic dualism, which positioned matter and spirit, body and soul in opposition, became paramount in the three scriptural religions. In such a context values such as the love of God, faith, and trust became paramount, while anything that involved physical activity was regarded as spiritually inferior, emphasizing the distance between man and God rather than bringing them together.

The traditional Jewish concept of mitzvah (precept, commandment) demanded physical action. The list of 613 such commandments, which every Jew was required to perform (or, in case of prohibitions, abstain from performing) hardly included any purely spiritual demand. Even prayer was not regarded as properly performed unless one's lips moved during recitation. Judaism thus had an image, and a self-image, of being an earthly, physical practice, remote from pure divine spirituality. Jewish theologians, deeply aware of this contradiction between their tradition and the spiritual norms in which they believed, sought ways of emphasizing the spiritual aspect of Judaism. From the beginning of the Middle Ages, Jewish rationalistic philosophers developed systems of *taamey mitzvot*, "reasons of the commandments." They pointed out the nonphysical reasons for complying with the ancient demands, discovering new layers of meaning in rituals and social requirements. In medieval Germany, the Jewish pietists developed a system that emphasized the aspect of spiritual trial in every commandment. They maintained that the physical instructions were difficulties that God presented on the path of individuals trying to achieve spiritual perfection. By subjugating their physicality to divine commandments the righteous achieve the spiritual goal of obedience to God and overcoming earthly desires. Both the rationalists and the pietists thus denigrated the importance of the physical commandment and attributed its religious meaning to the underlying spiritual significance of its performance.

The kabbalists developed a system that had similar results, but one that carried with it unusual spiritual power and became dominant in Judaism. Prayers and other rituals, physical and social demands, ethical deeds, and every other aspect of religious practice was associated by the kabbalists with the dynamic concepts that they developed concerning processes in the divine realms. From the late thirteenth century, the subject of *taamey mitzvot* became a central, and often dominant, one in kabbalistic literature. It is a central message of the Zohar, and almost every section of this vast work includes one or another interpretation of a commandment in light of the needs and demands of the divine powers. This put in the center of the kabbalistic worldview a powerful concept of interdependence between man and God, in which the commandments were the instruments used by man in order to influence the processes of the divine world, and ultimately shape his own fate.

The mythical processes that dominate this interaction are described in the Zohar and later works as being based on one dynamic aspect of the divine world. It is usually called the *shefa*, the flow of divine spirituality from the extreme, highest stages in the divine world down to the lower divine powers, and then to even lower realms, those of the archangels and angels, and finally the material world and to human beings. This divine flow is the necessary sustenance of all existence, even of the divine emanations themselves. Nothing can exist without deriving spiritual power from this divine flow. When this flow is diminished, the existence of every being is weakened. The upper realm may still derive its due from this flow, but lower strata of creation are deprived and threatened. According to the Zoharic myth of the dynamic world of the *sefirot*, the situation is always in flux: the right side may become stronger or weaker, and at the same time the realms on the left, of evil, may become stronger. The positions of the various powers are not fixed; they may become more elevated and thus closer to the origin of the *shefa*, or slide lower, receiving less divine flow. The masculine and feminine aspects of the divine world sometimes get closer to each other, thus increasing divine harmony and the flow of the *shefa*, or they may move apart, diminishing the divine flow. When the *shefa* flows in abundance, the good powers are stronger, whereas when it is diminished the powers of evil become stronger and their hold and dominance over the material world increase.

The decisive factor that determines to a very large extent the flow of this divine sustenance is, according to the Zohar, the behavior of human beings, the people of Israel. Righteous deeds of man increase the divine flow, tilting divine harmony to the right side, away from evil. Thus, any benevolent social act of charity and justice, every prayer said with devotion and proper intention, any compliance with the physical and ritualistic commandments, any avoidance of temptation and rejecting of sin and evil thoughts, enhances the divine flow. Sins, injustice, evil thoughts, unethical behavior, transgressions of the divine commands all diminish the *shefa's* flow, weakening existence, strengthening the evil powers, and increasing suffering and wickedness in the created world. The proper observance of the Sabbath, for instance, brings the *shekhinah* and her divine husband close together, even to erotic union, which exerts the greatest positive influence over the divine flow and brings bliss and harmony to the divine and material worlds alike. If the Sabbath is not properly observed, the opposite occurs:

the masculine and feminine powers are separated, the harmony is disturbed, the divine flow diminishes, and the lower worlds are deprived of their sustenance.

The commandments thus are deprived from their immediate, earthly context and relegated into the dynamic myth of the processes in the divine realms. God did not give human beings these commandments in order to achieve any earthly purpose. What God demands of man is participation in the vast drama of the dynamic occurrences in the divine world. The fate of the divine powers is thus relegated to the hands of human beings. Their well-being is decided by people's religious, social, and ethical behavior. Ultimately, however, it is the people who benefit from their obedience to divine commandments, because the increase of divine flow causes harmony and quiet on earth as well, rescuing the Jews from persecutions and enhancing the well-being of every individual, both in this world and in the world to come.

It is very difficult to find a parallel to this radical concept of interdependence between human beings and divine powers. It is certainly a dramatic spiritualization of religious life, for the physical commandments are described as having enormous spiritual impact on the highest realms of divine powers. The dynamic variations of the *shefa* give every individual an almost magical power to influence developments in the divine world. This impact is sometimes called theurgy, indicating the power of man to dominate the behavior and welfare of the divine powers. Indirectly, by observing the commandments a person decides his own fate together with those of the universe and the divine realms. The commandments are thus conceived as instruments that wield enormous spiritual power, shaping the fate of everything above and below. Instead of being an embarrassing heritage from ancient times, kabbalistic thinkers transformed the mitzvot into the expression of a unique spiritual force that dominates all aspects of human and divine existence.

Some indications of these conceptions may be found, in a vague and imprecise way, in pre-Zoharic kabbalistic works.

Since the Zohar, however, they became universal in the literature of the kabbalah and the most important and meaningful message that kabbalists conveyed to nonkabbalists. Some kabbalists composed manuals that explained the spiritual message of each commandment in detail, and later, since the sixteenth century, a distinct literary genre developed—kabbalistic ethical literature—that described the impact of every human deed on the world of the *sefirot*. It should be emphasized, however, that as a rule (with a few exceptions) the kabbalists did not demand knowledge, or even awareness, of the significance of the commandments in order to make them effective. Prayer, charity, observance, purity, and other acts carried their power within themselves, independent of the intention and understanding of the person performing them. The kabbalah, thus, did not compel people to follow particular practices in order to achieve a meaningful religious status. Yet kabbalists did convey the message that the highest levels of religious perfection cannot be attained except by people who are aware of the meaning and purpose of the commandments. This was often presented as the contemplation of the spiritual meaning of deeds, sometimes called *kavanot*, spiritual intentions that accompany the performance of the physical commandments.

Since the seventeenth century, this theurgical conception of the commandments was enhanced and reformulated by the forceful idea of the *tikkun* in the Lurianic kabbalah. The Zohar itself did present some connection between this system and the achievement of final, messianic redemption, but the Lurianic kabbalah made it its central message, which was then embraced by Judaism as a whole. The myth developed within the framework of Lurianic teachings presented the *tikkun* as the process that will redeem first and foremost the divine powers from the results of the primordial catastrophe called the breaking of the vessels. When the vessels are mended, divine perfection will signal the achievement of universal perfection. The only weapons people have in the struggle against the evil powers that dominate the universe are those of the commandments and ethical behavior. Following the divine demands signifies overcoming the physical and evil within man, and thus denotes the spiritual victory of good over evil. The accumulation of such minute victories enhances the completion of the *tikkun*, while sins and transgressions strengthen the evil powers and delay the achievement of redemption. Here again, knowledge of the mythical significance of the commandments is helpful, but not a necessity: the power of redemption is inherent in the deeds themselves, and the theurgic impact of their performance is automatic. Every person, every deed, every moment is integrated in the vast mythical project of the *tikkun*, whether they know and wish it or not. One cannot resign from this cosmic struggle; such a resignation constitutes a sin, which empowers the satanic forces.

It should be emphasized that these theurgic concepts, both in the Zoharic system and in the Lurianic kabbalah, constitute a formidable conservative power, despite their appearance as radical, revolutionary new ideas. The dynamic system of the *sefirot*, the myth of the breaking of the vessels and the *tikkun*, and especially the dependence of the divine powers on human religious deeds are new, unexpected, somewhat unsettling images in a Jewish context. Yet the bottom-line message is purely a conservative one. If one accepts and internalizes these new conceptions, what should one now do? How shall one conduct one's daily life? The answer is, one should do what one was commanded to do anyway, independent of the kabbalistic theories. One should pray devoutly, pursue social justice, help the poor, observe the Sabbath and other holidays, observe the laws concerning kosher food and physical cleanliness—everything that a nonkabbalist is obligated to do just because this is what the halakhah demands. Medieval and modern kabbalah never offered any spiritual shortcuts, any recipe for spiritual achievement without strictly observing the tedious daily observance of the multitude of the mitzvot. The flowing of the *shefa* and the process of the *tikkun* cannot be achieved but by the strict adherence to the instruments supplied by God in the Torah for this purpose. These systems prohibit any change or deviation from the traditional modes of religious adherence, because the commandments, being divinely devised instruments for the achievement of divine goals, cannot be tempered by the logic or inclinations of human beings. The most minute deviation from the halakhah immediately and automatically constitutes a transgression, thus inevitably strengthening the powers of evil and delaying the completion of the *tikkun*. The kabbalists thus presented a radical new mythology, which drastically spiritualized Jewish religious culture, but at the same time they enhanced and invigorated the traditional Jewish way of life, giving it powerful new spiritual incentives.

Spiritualization did not mean departing from the physical, but rather reinterpreting the spiritual and giving the mundane, daily rituals a magnificent, new dimension of meaning. Adherence to the kabbalistic conceptions became synonymous in Jewish history to strict orthodoxy. The first thing that nineteenth-century reformers of Judaism did, before they began to modernize and change the halakhah and the prayerbook, was to rid themselves of any trace of reverence or regard for the teachings of the kabbalah. They understood that the kabbalah cannot be separated from the strict traditional observance of the totality of the commandments. Until the middle of the twentieth century, the Jewish denominations of reformed, conservative, reconstructionist, and modern orthodox were characterized by their rejection of any interest in the kabbalah. The rabbinic Jewish academic institutions in the United States did not accept, until very recently, the kabbalah as a legitimate aspect of Jewish culture, while secular academic institutions in the United States, Israel, and Europe did not have any such hesitations.

7   The *Kabbalah Denudata* was an extensive anthology of kabbalistic works for the Christian world.

5

Modern Times I:
The Christian Kabbalah

The kabbalah was transformed from a uniquely Jewish religious tradition into a European concept, integrated with Christian theology, philosophy, science, and magic, at the end of the fifteenth century. From that time to the present it has continued its dual existence as a Jewish phenomenon on the one hand and as a component of European culture on the other hand. The failure to distinguish between the two different—actually, radically different—meanings of the kabbalah in the intrinsic Jewish context and in the European-Christian context is a key reason for the confusion surrounding the term and concept of the kabbalah today. Readers are disappointed when they do not find the characteristics of the Jewish kabbalah in the writings of Christian kabbalists, and vice versa. The confusion is increased by the fact that there is no unanimity in the usage of the term either within Judaism or outside of it, so that various, different and conflicting conceptions of what the kabbalah is prevail in both cultures. The following paragraphs are not intended to explain what the kabbalah—or even the Christian kabbalah—"really" is. They constitute an attempt to present the main outlines of the development of the different meanings and attitudes that contributed to the multiple faces of the kabbalah in European (and, later, American) Christian culture.

The development of the Christian kabbalah began in the school of Marsilio Ficino in Florence, in the second half of the fifteenth century. It was the peak of the Italian Renaissance, when Florence was governed by the Medici family, who supported and encouraged philosophy, science, and art. Florence was a gathering place for many of the greatest minds of Europe, among them refugees from Constantinople, which was conquered by the Turks in 1453. Ficino is best known for his translations of Plato's writings from Greek to Latin, but of much importance was his translation to Latin of the corpus of esoteric, mysterious old treatises known as the Hermetica. These works, probably originating from Egypt in late antiquity, are attributed to a mysterious ancient philosopher, Hermes Trismegestus (The Thrice-Great Hermes), and they deal with magic, astrology, and esoteric theology. Ficino and his followers found in these and other works a new source for innovative speculations, which centered around the concept of magic as an ancient scientific doctrine, the source of all religious and natural truth.

A great thinker who emerged from this school was Count Giovani Pico dela Mirandola, a young scholar and theologian, who died at age thirty-three in 1496.Pico took a keen interest in the Hebrew language, and had Jewish scholars as friends and teachers. He began to study the kabbalah both in Hebrew and in translations to Latin made for him by a Jewish convert to Christianity, Flavius Mithredates. His best-known work, the "Nine Hundred Theses," included numerous theses that were based on the kabbalah, and he famously proclaimed that Christianity's truth is best demonstrated by the disciplines of magic and kabbalah. Modern scholars have found it difficult to distinguish in Pico's works between these two: magic is often presented as a synonym for the kabbalah. Pico regarded magic as a science, both in the natural and theological realms, and he interpreted the kabbalistic texts with which he was familiar as ancient esoteric lore, conserved by the Jews, at the heart of which was the Christian message, which is fortified by the study of kabbalah.

Pico's work was continued by his disciple, the German philosopher and linguist Johannes Reuchlin, who lived from 1455 to 1522. Reuchlin acquired an impressive knowledge of Hebrew and of kabbalistic texts, which was expressed in numerous works, but mainly in his *De Arte kabbalistica* (1516), which became the textbook on the subject for two centuries. This work presents, in three parts, the philosophical, theological, and scientific discussions of three scholars, a Christian, a Muslim, and a Jew. The Jewish scholar is named Simon, and he is introduced as a descendant of the family of Rabbi Shimeon bar Yohai, the central figure in the narratives of the Zohar. Simon presents the principles of the kabbalah (as Reuchlin saw them), and his Christian and Muslim colleagues integrate them with general principles of philosophy—represented mainly by what they believed to be Pythagorean philosophy—and those of science and magic. Reuchlin's presentation was regarded by his own disciples and by followers throughout Europe as a definitive, authoritative presentation of the kabbalah.

"Kabbalah" in the writings of Pico and Reuchlin is radically different from the medieval Jewish kabbalah that they used as their source. They included in this term all postbiblical Jewish works, including the Talmud and midrash, the medieval rationalistic philosophers including Maimonides, and the writings of many Jewish exegetes of the Bible, most of them having no relationship to the kabbalah. The Jewish esoteric texts that they read, in the original or in translation, included many nonkabbalistic ones, including those of the Hasidey Ashkenaz (the medieval Jewish pietist) or of Abraham Abulafia, which were not typical of the mainstream of Jewish kabbalah. The Zohar was used very seldom, and the references to it were often derived from quotations in other works. The image of "kabbalah" as it emerges from the works of early Christian kabbalists is thus meaningfully different from the one presented by the Hebrew sources.

Most meaningful are the differences in the subjects that are discussed. The intense kabbalistic contemplation of the "secret of creation" and the emergence of the system of the *sefirot* from the infinite Godhead is rather marginal in the deliberations of the Christian scholars; they had ready the theology of the Trinity, which they integrated with their understanding of the kabbalah. The *shekhinah* as a feminine power was of little interest, as well as the erotic metaphorical portrayal of the relationships in the divine world. The dualism of good and evil in the Zoharic kabbalah was not a main subject, nor was the theurgic element and the impact of the performance of the commandments on celestial processes. Mystical experiences, visions, and spiritual elevations were not at the center of their interest; they regarded themselves as scholars, scientists, and philosophers rather than mystics.

The Christian kabbalists were most impressed by the Jewish nonsemantic treatment of language, for which they had no Christian counterpart. The various names of God and the celestial powers were for them a new revelation. The various transmutations of the Hebrew alphabet, as well as the numerological methodologies, which are essentially midrashic rather than kabbalistic, became the center of their speculations. The Hebrew concept of language as an expression of infinite divine wisdom contrasted with the intensely semantic Christian attitude toward scriptures, which was the result of their being translations, and this disparity is essential to the understanding of the Christian kabbalists. In many cases, like that of "numerology," it was the methodologies of the midrash that became the core of their understanding of the "kabbalah." The freedom of speculation and the ease with which new meanings can be attributed to ancient texts in this context were their main concerns. A prominent example of the identification of the kabbalah with magic and numerology was presented in the popular, influential work *De Occulta Philosophia* (1531), by Cornelius Agrippa of Nettesheim, who was secretary to the Emperor Charles V.

8   Henry More's *Vision of Ezekiel*. Many thinkers in the Cambridge
school of neo-Platonists such as Henry More studied the kabbalah.

The meeting with the Jewish conception of divine language enabled the Christian kabbalists to adopt the belief in the ability of language—especially names, and in particular divine names—to influence reality. This gave the sanction of ancient authority to the Renaissance scholars' belief in magic as a dominant power in the universe. What was commonplace in Judaism (and was not conceived of as magic) became prominent in the Christian kabbalists' worldview. This was easily combined with the other major conception that these scholars derived from the Jewish sources—*harmonia mundi*. This image of the parallel strata that create structural harmony in the cosmos, nature, and human beings derived from the Sefer Yezira, which in the kabbalah was extended to the divine realm, was thus integrated into European philosophy and science. One of the most important expressions of this is found in the works of the Venetian scholar Francesco Giorgio (1460–1541), especially in his well-known *De Harmonia Mundi* (1525). The Hebrew works were not the only, nor even the major, source of this Christian concept of *hamonia mundi*; the relationships between microcosmos and macrocosmos, and between man and the Creator in whose image he was created, were developed in various schools of neo-Platonists during the Middle Ages. Yet in the schools of Pico, Reuchlin, and their successors they were often described as elements of the kabbalah, the ancient Jewish tradition that Moses received on Mount Sinai.

Among the famous thinkers of the sixteenth century who made the kabbalah a major subject of their studies was Guillaume Postel of Paris (1510–1581), who was the first to publish the Sefer Yezira with a Latin translation and a commentary; he also translated several sections from the Zohar. Lurianic kabbalah was first presented to the Christian world in an extensive anthology of kabbalistic works, *Kabbala Denudata* (1677–1684) compiled by Christian Knorr von Rosenroth. The works of the great seventeenth-century German mystic Jacob Boehme were interpreted by his followers as reflecting kabbalistic concepts. In England, some thinkers in the Cambridge school of neo-Platonists—Henry More and Robert Fludd, among many others—used the kabbalah. In Holland, the numerous works of the theologian Franciscus Mercurius van Helmont, reflect an extensive use of kabbalistic materials, and it seems that he collaborated in this field with Gottfried Wilhelm Leibnitz (1646–1716). In many of these and other works the speculations based on kabbalistic ideas were integrated with astrological theories and especially alchemical ones, presenting the kabbalah as one of those occult doctrines. Gershom Scholem described the work of the German philosopher Franz Josef Molitor (1779–1861) on the philosophy of tradition as "the crowning and final achievement of the Christian kabbalah."

Since the seventeenth century, kabbalah, in different spellings, became a common term in European languages, indicating in an imprecise manner anything that was ancient, mysterious, magical, and to some extent dangerous. It became an adjective that was used in various ways, often without any clear connection to either the Hebrew sources or even the original works of the Christian kabbalists. "Cabal" was used to describe a secret group of people contemplating mischief. During the Enlightenment interest in this esoteric, magical doctrine diminished, but it returned forcefully with the renewed attention to myths and secrets in the nineteenth century. References to the kabbalah are found in popular, pseudoscientific works, as well as in treatises dedicated to various forms of mysticism.

One of the most meaningful results of development of the Christian kabbalah was the separation between kabbalah and Judaism; these two terms could not be regarded as necessarily dependent on each other. In Christian culture, one can be an adherent of the kabbalah without being Jewish, and it is even possible to combine kabbalah and anti-Semitism. Carl Gustav Jung could thus combine admiration of the kabbalah with enmity toward Jewish culture. When this sense of the separateness of the kabbalah returned to Jewish context, in the late nineteenth century and more intensely during the twentieth century, it sanctioned a division between kabbalah and Jewish orthodoxy and observance of the commandments. Adherence to kabbalah became a substitute for the acceptance of Jewish tradition as a whole. This enabled people to perceive themselves as being connected to Jewish traditional culture without observing the elements of the tradition that they rejected.

Whereas the early reformers of Judaism in the nineteenth century found the spiritual dimension of Judaism through adherening to rationalism and social ethics, groups of Jews who sought a nonorthodox spiritual, yet traditional, type of Judaism tended to adopt kabbalah, or what they believed to be kabbalah, as a central aspect of their worldview and religious rituals. This was evident, for instance, in some secular kibbutzim in Israel that vigorously rejected the orthodox way of life, but introduced kabbalistic terms, images, and rituals into their culture, representing their ties to Jewish cultural tradition. A similar phenomenon was prominent among the *havurot* (the Hebrew word for "groups") of young Jews in the United States in the 1960s and 1970s; kabbalah was often combined with some neo-Hasidic expressions, endowing their spiritual experiences with an aura of Jewish traditionalism while de-emphasizing, or even rejecting outright, the authority of the halakhah. Since the 1980s these groups and tendencies were integrated with the atmosphere of the New Age culture. Adherence to some elements of kabbalistic terminology enabled these *havurot* to develop a Jewish identity without the obligation to observe the strict rules of Jewish orthodoxy. The kabbalah was thus established as a traditional Jewish substitute to the attractions of Zen Buddhism, Transcendental Meditation, and other alternative religions and spiritual practices. In many cases the kabbalah was identified with these and other spiritual fashions that originated in the East and became an integrated component of European and American culture, especially among students and young academics on university campuses, where young Jews assembled in quest for spiritual identity. The term "kabbalah" did not carry the reservations and ambiguous attitudes that non-Jews had toward the term "Judaism" and the traditional expressions of Jewish orthodoxy.

9 According to Lurianic thought, the structure of the ten sefirot also represents the basic structural characteristic of everything that exists, be it spiritual or material.

6

Modern Times II:
Safed and the Lurianic Kabbalah

Following the destruction of the great Jewish center in the Ibe-
rian peninsula in 1492, groups of Jewish intellectuals gradually
congregated in the small town of Safed in the Upper Galilee,
attracted by the traditional belief that Rabbi Shimeon bar Yohai,
the main figure of the Zohar, was buried in the nearby village
of Miron. The Jewish community in Safed was very small (hardly
two thousand families in the sixteenth century), but it included
many of the most inspired and ambitions minds of the period.
A pioneering spirit imbued the community, which believed itself to be the religious leader of the Jewish people. In the 1530s
the town's scholars were engaged in a revolutionary endeavor.
They intended to reconstitute the traditional ordination of rabbis, which started with Moses on Mount Sinai and continued
through biblical and talmudic times but was discontinued in
the beginning of the Middle Ages, when it was relegated to the
realm of messianic redemption. The Safed scholars believed
that they should actively prepare for the redemption, and the
renewed *semikhah* (ordination) was carried out there for several generations. The rabbis of Jerusalem and Egypt did not
accept it, and it seems that the venture ended in failure.

Rabbi Jacob Berav was the leader of the movement, and
one his ordained students, Rabbi Joseph Karo, is the author of
the most normative and dominant work of religious law in

modern Judaism—the *Shulhan Arukh* (The Laid Table). Karo was a kabbalist as well as a lawyer, and he wrote an extensive kabbalistic work that he claimed was dictated by a divine messenger, a *magid*, whom he regarded as a manifestation of the *shekhinah*. Several great writers, all of them kabbalists, were active in Safed, among them Rabbi Shlomo Alkabetz, Rabbi Moshe Alsheikh, and the greatest kabbalist of the time—Rabbi Moshe Cordovero, who wrote numerous kabbalistic treatises in addition to his multivolume commentary on the Zohar, *Or Yakar* (Precious Light).

The community of Safed distinguished itself by strict adherence to the ethical and ritualistic commandments, believing that scrupulous observance would enhance the arrival of the era of redemption. They developed a sense of communal interdependence: religious perfection was everyone's endeavor, and anyone who transgressed harmed not only his own soul but hurt everybody by delaying the redemption. They organized several "repentance groups," in which the members would consult and assist each other in striving for religious and ethical achievements. The very concept of repentance underwent a radical transformation: it no longer represented the return to observance after a transgression, but a way of life, one of complete dedication to extreme orthodoxy, repenting not only one's own sins but the sins of all others, past and present. The conception seems to have been that God does not deal only with individuals, but with the people as a whole, and redemption is to be achieved by communal or even national perfection. Each individual is religiously responsible for the sins and transgressions of everyone else, living and dead, and therefore there cannot be any limit to the sacrifices and efforts of repentance. Several Safed scholars went as far as inflicting themselves with pain and wounds, including self-immolation, which is very rare in Jewish practice.

Isaac Luria, who revolutionized the kabbalah in this period, arrived in Safed in 1570 when these practices were at their peak. He was born in Safed in 1534, but his family migrated to Egypt, where he grew up and acquired his traditional and kabbalistic education. When he returned to Safed a group of disciples assembled around him. Rabbi Hayyim Vital Klippers, who was already a well-known Safed scholar, headed the disciples, who believed that Luria's soul was often uplifted to the divine realms, where he studied great secrets in the celestial academy of Torah. Although we have a few fragments of his writing discussing portions from the Zohar, he did not write much. He explained his reluctance to write by the enormity of the visions that were before his eyes. It was like a great river, he is reported as saying, which he could not control and let it flow from his tiny pen. Luria died in a plague two years after his return to Safed, in 1572, at the age of thirty-eight. Some of his disciples explained his early death as punishment for revealing forbidden secrets, thus enhancing the prestige of his teachings. Others maintained that he was the Messiah Son of Joseph, the commander of God's armies who was destined to die just before the Messiah Son of David redeems the world. (Rabbi Hayyim Vital believed this second role to be his, and he asserted that Luria had revealed to him his own messianic destiny.) Luria's prestige grew in the next decades, a body of hagiographic tales relating his miraculous knowledge was told by those who knew him, and his disciples assembled his teachings in several versions.

The most important studies of Luria's teachings were presented by Gershom Scholem and Isaiah Tishby in 1941, and since then, while we have many books and articles dealing with particular problems and aspects of Luria's teachings, the main picture that they drew is still dominant. Further studies may cast some doubts, but as of now presenting their studies is the best that we can do. The reader should not accept the following description as a final word; it may be revised, but today we do not have any comprehensive alternative.

The Withdrawal: *Zimzum* and *Shevirah*

Isaac Luria dared, unlike most theologians and philosophers, to put in the center of his worldview the most basic questions, which are so often avoided: Why everything? Why does God exist? Why did the creation occur? What is meaning of everything? He gave to these questions a most radical and revolutionary answer, expressed in daring mythological concepts and terms. The most innovative concept that lies at the heart of Luria's teachings is the imperfection of beginning. Existence does not begin with a perfect Creator bringing into being an imperfect universe; rather, the existence of the universe is the result of an inherent flaw or crisis within the infinite Godhead, and the purpose of creation is to correct it.

The initial stage in the emergence of existence is described by the Lurianic myth as a negative one: the withdrawal of the infinite divine *ein sof* from a certain "place" in order to bring about "empty space" in which the process of creation could proceed. The Lurianic mystics called this process *zimzum* (constriction), a term taken from talmudic literature indicating the constriction of the *shekhinah* in the space between the images of the angels on the holy ark in the temple in Jerusalem. Here, however, it is not constriction into a space but withdrawal from a space, creating what Luria called, in Aramaic, *tehiru* (emptiness). Into this empty region a line of divine light began to shine, gradually taking the shape of the structure of the divine emanations, the *sefirot*.

Luria made use of a concept developed a generation before him by Moses Cordovero, who attempted to explain the individuality and functional differences between the divine emanations. The question he addressed was: if the *sefirot* are divine, how can they be different from each other? There cannot be differentiation within divine perfection. His response was: the *sefirot* are to be conceived like vessels (*kelim*); the essence within them is pure divine light, while the vessels are "made" of somewhat courser divine light, which gives them "shapes," expressing their individuality and specific functions. This is reminiscent of the Aristotelian concept of the matter and form of which everything is made; yet Aristotle ascribed a higher spiritual position to form compared to matter, whereas Cordovero did the opposite. For him, the inner essence was more elevated than the surrounding shape of the vessels.

When the "straight line" of divine light poured into the *tehiru*, the "empty space," it began to draw circles and shapes, bringing "vessels" into existence, and then pouring the pure divine essence into them. At this point, a great catastrophe occurred: the vessels could not contain the immense flow of divine light, and the seven lower ones broke, their shards falling down and the inner essence ascending and returning to its source. This is called in Lurianic terminology "the breaking of the vessels" (*shevirat ha-kelim*), expressing the concept that the initial attempt by the Godhead to establish the system of emanated divine powers failed, resulting in a state of destruction and crisis within the divine realm.

The meaning of the *shevirah* is the most esoteric subject in Lurianic teachings, discussed only in very few passages in the writings of the disciples, and even these few texts present different conceptions. It is a paradox that can be very destructive for religious thought: the supreme divine power undertook an endeavor, and failed to carry it out. Such a catastrophe, at the foundation of existence, has to be explained. The analysis presented by Scholem and Tishby is most profound and mythic in character. According to it, when the initial phase, the *zimzum*, was carried out, the empty space was not really empty. It is like when a container is emptied of water; the inside of the container is still wet, with water clinging to its sides. Some divine light remained in the *tehiru*, and this residue, called by the Lurianists, in Aramaic, *reshimu* (impression) included in it some elements of difference and "otherness" that previously were scattered within the infinite Godhead. This was the real purpose of the *zimzum*: to concentrate and discharge these potentially different entities away from the Godhead, thus achieving uniformity and perfection for the rest. This task has been accomplished successfully in the process of the *zimzum*. This can be seen as a cathartic process within the eternal *ein sof*.

The second stage, the pouring of divine light into the *tehiru* and the formation of the vessels was intended to achieve a more radical purpose: the transforming of these different elements into positive, constructive entities. Had the *reshimu* participated in the endeavor of forming the divine emanations, its difference would have been eliminated, because it took part in the process together with the rest of the divine light. The otherness in the *reshimu* was intended to supply the positive difference between the essence and the vessels, supplying the divine powers with their individual features. The *shevirah* was the result of the refusal, or rebellion, of the *reshimu* elements, which caused the breaking of the vessels and established a separate realm in the lower part of the *tehiru*, a realm marked by destruction and rebelliousness. Their potential difference was thus actualized, and the domain they established can now be characterized as the realm of evil, dominated by the powers that oppose creation.

It is evident that Luria conceived the eternal, infinite Godhead that preceded these processes to be imperfect, with the origins of evil deeply imbedded in it in a potential manner. It is very rare that theologians and mystics view the origins of evil as completely divine and eternal. The dualism presented here has nothing to do with humanity and its sinfulness, because it existed long before they came to be. Existence—even divine existence—is not the source of evil; rather, everything was emanated and created within the framework of divine attempts to rid itself from this dualism and bring about, for the first time, divine perfection and unity.

The Lurianic narrative continues and portrays everything that happened after the *shevirah* as divine attempts to overcome and correct that initial catastrophe. Divine light poured again and formed the system of the *sefirot*, and the lower worlds were created. The creation of Adam in the Garden of Eden was again an attempt to overcome dualism: Adam was created as a dual entity, including within him the elements of good and evil. If

Adam had obeyed God, good would have triumphed over evil and the cosmic and divine dualism would have been abolished. However, when Adam transgressed, the opposite happened: the *shevirah* occurred again, the evil powers were strengthened. God then chose a people, the people of Israel, to carry on the struggle to dispose of evil. They were almost successful when they assembled near Mount Sinai to accept the Torah. Then they transgressed when they worshipped the golden calf, and again a *shevirah* occurred, and so on, throughout history.

The Correction: *Tikkun*

These attempts to correct the primordial catastrophe are designated in Lurianic terminology by the most powerful concept that this school introduced—the *tikkun* (the mending [of the broken vessels]). The *tikkun* is the purpose of creation, of human existence, of the Torah, and of the people of Israel. The achievement of the *tikkun* is the ultimate redemption, bringing perfection first and foremost to God himself, and as a result—to the universe, to humanity, and to the people of Israel. The instruments of achieving this are dedication and absorption in the observance of the mitzvot, complete commitment to the norms of ethical behavior, and unselfish pursuit of religious perfection for every person, for every community, and for the people as a whole. It can be described as a nationalistic ideology, setting an all-encompassing collective goal in which everyone should participate to the full extent of his abilities. The arsenal, the means by which this endeavor can be carried out, is the Torah, the halakhah, and the totality of Jewish tradition. Thus, while the concepts and terms of the Lurianic myth can be conceived as strange or even heretical, the practical message of this mythology is an ultraorthodox one. A believer in the *tikkun* does not deviate from Jewish traditional orthodoxy. Rather, he pursues the same goals with increased dedication, because he knows the grand, ultimate purpose of his efforts, the cosmic consequences of his deeds or misdeeds. The *tikkun* is the purpose of the existence of the divine realms, of creation as a whole, and the awareness that performance of the commandments means fulfilling a vital role in this process gave a new impetus to the observance of the traditional religious tasks. The intense dualism of this myth made every Jew a soldier in the battle of good against evil.

A meaningful metaphor was placed in the center of the Lurianic conception of the *tikkun*: the captive divine sparks that have to be redeemed by human deeds. When the breaking of the vessels and subsequent catastrophes occurred, most of the pure divine essence in the vessels escaped and ascended back to its divine source. But, many divine sparks remained enclosed by the shards of the vessels, and they are kept captive by the evil powers governing the lower realms. These sparks are not only in exile, removed from their proper place, they also supply the evil powers with divine sustenance. According to the Lurianic worldview, existence is derived only from the good divine light; nothing can exist for even a moment without deriving its power from a good divine source. (This, actually, is a transformed version of the old neo-Platonic identification of light and spirituality with existence, denying the real, independent existence of evil.) If all the sparks are uplifted and returned to their proper place in the upper divine realms, evil will have no source of divine light and it will cease to exist.

The process of *tikkun* is therefore one of separation: uplifting sparks separates the good from evil, thus causing the abolishment of evil. Sparks are released when a person performs a commandment, says a prayer, eats a kosher meal, observes the Sabbath, or performs an act of charity and justice. On the other hand, every transgression and sin, any ethical misdeed, causes a spark from the person's divine soul to fall captive to the powers of evil, thus strengthening them. Redemption will occur when all the sparks have been uplifted and separated from evil, which means, actually, when all the people observe the commandments and ethical norms and refrain from any transgression and injustice. A person can never know whether the spark he is uplifting at this moment is the last one, bringing about the redemption, or whether the transgression he has just committed has prevented the completion of the *tikkun* and thus delayed the redemption. Every moment, every deed, can be the crucial, final one, deciding the fate of the universe. Collective responsibility is paramount: what is at stake is not the fate of an individual soul, but that of the state of all creation.

This tremendous burden is borne by every individual, at all times. It is democratic in the sense that the scholar and the ignorant, the Lurianic mystic and the unschooled laborer participate in it and share the responsibility. People whose souls are derived from a higher source in the divine realm may have more influence, but without everybody participating in the *tikkun* it is bound to fail. Lurianism, therefore, despite its total dedication to the process of redemption, is not messianic in the literal sense of the term. The messiah does not have any particular role to play in bringing about the redemption. Until all the sparks have been uplifted, he is a participant in the endeavor like everybody else. Only after the *tikkun* is achieved, his position will be recognized and he will be crowned the King of the Universe. Rabbi Hayyim Vital, Luria's greatest disciple, believed himself to be the messiah and wrote a personal diary, *Sefer ha-Hezyonot* (The Book of Visions), in which he described his experiences and the evidence for his unique future role. Yet, he did not express a belief that this role required any particular action, and did not demand a role of leadership beside his position as the writer of his teacher's ideas. The commandments are known to everybody, the ways by which sparks can be uplifted are described in detail in traditional Jewish law and ethics. The messiah has no specific role, or, to put it in another way, the Lurianic kabbalah, like previous kabbalistic schools, did not create a concept of religious or mystical leadership. This task was reserved for the next century, to the messianic movement around Shabbatai Zevi.

On the practical religious level Lurianism was clearly orthodox and traditional, yet it did innovate and establish several new rituals that had an impact on Jewish daily observance. A new prayer book, which included many quotations from the Zohar and kabbalistic hymns, began to spread in the Jewish world and was used by people who wished to dedicate themselves to the task of the *tikkun* with particular zeal. Customs that instituted special sessions of prayer and study at designated times became the recognized characteristics of Lurianic adherence; they were called *tikkun*, and were conducted at midnight (*tikkun hazot*) or the night of the holiday of Shavuot (*tikkun leyl shavuot*).

The teachings of Luria spread gradually throughout the Jewish world in the first decades of the seventeenth century, carried not only by kabbalistic manuscripts but also by popular ethical treatises and collections of hagiographic narratives concerning Luria and his disciples. Rabbi Hayyim Vital tried to preserve the esoteric character of Luria's teachings and prohibited their being copied and distributed, but despite his efforts the message spread. It gradually replaced the kabbalah of Moshe Cordovero, and dominates Jewish theology to this very day. Since Luria, no traditional, orthodox alternative worldview has been presented within Judaism. The Lurianic prayer book gradually became the standard one in most Jewish communities. Lurianic kabbalists reinterpreted all the ancient sources, from the Bible to the Zohar, as reflecting and expressing the Lurianic doctrines.

Unlike the medieval kabbalah, Lurianic teachings did not remain in the domain of small closed groups but became the subject of popular preaching, written and oral, and penetrated all aspects of Jewish culture. Jews did not become mystics in the seventeenth, eighteenth, and nineteenth centuries Rather, the Lurianic myth helped explain the exile and the way to achieve national and individual redemption, and as such it became a "national" religious ideology. The great upheavals in

Jewish religious thought and practice, including the emergence of Sabbatian messianism in the seventeenth century and the modern Hasidic movement in the eighteenth, can be viewed as changes of emphasis and modifications of Lurianic theology. Even today, in the ultraorthodox Jewish communities, Lurianism is unchallenged. Other Jewish spiritual and religious movements, such as the enlightenment, reform, and Zionism, are regarded by the traditionalists as external and irrelevant if not evil. More than four hundred years after it came into being, the Lurianic myth is alive and dominant.

Subsequent kabbalists discussed, interpreted, and transformed Lurianic ideas, but the main concept—the *tikkun*—remained unchanged. The concept of the *shevirah* was relatively marginalized, but the *zimzum* was discussed and its character has been changed. Several prominent kabbalists viewed the *zimzum* as a voluntary divine process intended to make divinity more approachable to the created realms and to the people. The *zimzum* was often conceived as an expression of divine benevolence, of God diminishing himself in order to be able to be perceived and understood by his creatures.

Outside of Judaism, in Christian Europe, the concept of the *tikkun* made no meaningful impression, but the term "*zimzum*" seems to have impressed several European thinkers, and it became a meaningful one within Christian kabbalah and other segments of European esotericism in the seventeenth and eighteenth centuries. Other aspects of Lurianic kabbalah may have had some relevance to the development of religious ideas in early modern Europe. One of them is the Lurianic concept that the structure of the ten *sefirot* is not only a description of the original ten divine hypostases, but they represent the basic structural characteristic of everything that exists, be it spiritual or material. The concept that the human soul reflects this structure is found in the writings of medieval kabbalists, but the Lurianic writers, especially Rabbi Hayyim Vital, extended it to include all aspects of existence. The ancient concept of *harmonia mundi* was extended by Vital to encompass the nature of creation as a whole. The intense individual characteristics of each *sefirah*, as portrayed in the Zohar, were submerged in this doctrine and transformed into principles that constitute the building blocks of every aspect of existence.

It is paradoxical that the core of the mythical description of the divine powers in the medieval kabbalah has been replaced in the Lurianic worldview by a kind of scientific system. The nature of each entity is decided not by its structure—because everything is made of the same components—but by its place in the detailed hierarchy of beings descending from the supreme Godhead to the animals and stones in a field. In order to define an entity one has to pinpoint its place and position: the element of *hod* within the realm of *keter* within the stage of *yesod* in this or that realm. The myth of *zimzum, shevirah,* and *tikkun* did not prevent Vital and others from describing existence in a quantitative, scientific hierarchy of identical elements identified by their relative position to each other. A similar attitude can be found in Vital's detailed discussion of the human soul.

The concept of reincarnation (*gilgul*) became central in the psychological doctrines of the Lurianic school, perhaps for the first time in the history of the kabbalah. There are five strata in the soul, reflecting the structure of the *sefirot*; each of these components has its own history, and each wanders from body to body, from generation to generation, independent of the other parts. Each soul, therefore, is a meeting of parts that have their own history and experiences. In his book of visions, Vital described the detailed history of his own soul, the soul of the messiah, which first came to existence in the body of Cain, and has been moving from body to body until it was re-collected in Vital's body. Vital claims that this information was given to him by Luria himself, whose greatness was expressed by his knowledge of the history of every soul.

These and other Lurianic concepts have occupied the deliberations of kabbalists for the last four hundred years. Yet the main message of Lurianism, which was embraced by Judaism as a whole, was the tension between exile and redemption, at the center of which stands every individual who seeks to strengthen the powers of good and weaken those of evil by his religious and ethical daily behavior. The sense of a unified fate and collective responsibility and waiting for the imminent completion of the *tikkun* and the beginning of the messianic age became paramount in Jewish culture. In the middle and second half of the seventeenth century these spiritual conceptions became a historical force that changed Judaism in the most fundamental way.

SABETHA SEBI
Vermeynden Meſſias Der Ioden

10 Born in Smyrna, Shabbatai Zevi was the great leader of the messianic movement who convinced many he was the messiah.

7

Modern Times III:
The Sabbatian Messianic Movement

The enormous burden that Lurianic teachings placed on every individual was characteristic of the pioneering, devoted community of spiritualists that dominated the unique culture of sixteenth-century Safed. When the teachings of Safed spread to Jewish communities throughout the world, ordinary people were faced with this extraordinary responsibility for the fate of God, the universe, and the Jewish people. This was very difficult to sustain, and during the messianic upheaval in the seventeenth century the concept of a mystical-messianic leader—a divine figure who could undertake a part of this responsibility and direct the people toward the completion of the *tikkun*—emerged. The person who brought about this meaningful modification of the Lurianic kabbalah was Nathan of Gaza, who is known in history as the prophet of the messiah Shabbatai Zevi.

Shabbatai Zevi was born in Smyrna, one of the great centers of Jewish culture in the Ottoman Empire, in 1626. He was versed in kabbalah, and during his youth he began to develop his messianic pretensions. There was nothing unusual in that; there were several people who believed in their own messianic destiny in most Jewish centers. He declared his mission; behaved in strange, provocative ways; and was disregarded, ridiculed, and often banished from various communities in Turkey and other countries in the Middle East. In 1665 he met in Gaza a young Lurianic kabbalist, twenty years his junior, who came to believe that Shabbatai Zevi was indeed the messiah. This young man, Nathan, described himself as a prophet and began to preach, in various ways, that the process of the *tikkun* had been completed and that the messiah had already appeared. He "discovered" ancient documents supporting this, and told about his visions concerning the arrival of the age of redemption. Most people who heard about his prophecy received it as authentic. There was nothing unusual in a person pretending to be a messiah, but the claim to prophecy, coming from the Holy Land, was a new experience for Jews. Because the Talmud states that there is no prophecy but in the land of Israel, they tended to listen and believe. Nathan's message was expressed in Lurianic, orthodox terms, and did not seem to include any element that aroused suspicion. His first pamphlet was a call for repentance, written in the most traditional and orthodox terms. During the year 1666, Nathan's messianic prophecy spread quickly from synagogue to synagogue, first in the Ottoman Empire and then Christian Europe. Many accepted it with great enthusiasm, and very few found any reason to hesitate. By the summer of 1666 it seemed that the whole Jewish world was in the grip of messianic fervor.

Nathan's endeavor only succeeded because it was an expression of the kabbalah's dominance in Jewish religious culture, and because of the eruption of messianic interest in Judaism following the crisis of the expulsion from Spain. The numerous leaders and thinkers who shaped the theologies of the scores of messianic groups active from 1666 to the beginning of the nineteenth century were all integrated in kabbalistic thinking, and in most cases in Lurianic kabbalah, which they developed according to their particular aspirations and needs. This was true not only for Jewish Sabbatians, as the followers of Shabbatai Zevi were known, but also included those who converted to Christianity and Islam, and continued to cherish their unique kabbalistic-messianic conceptions in the foreign cultural context.

In 1665–1666, Nathan of Gaza presented his adaptation of a kabbalistic terminology and worldview into Sabbatian messianism. His worldview was a modification of Lurianic kabbalah, introducing into the Safed system a new element, the role of the messiah in the process of the *tikkun*, the mending of the original catastrophe that made the world a realm ruled by evil. According to Nathan, it was not enough to follow the Lurianic precepts of utilizing religious ritual and observance to uplift the scattered sparks of divine light and return them to their proper place in the divine world. There is, he argued, a core of evil, which human beings cannot overcome on their own. In the kabbalistic anthropomorphic metaphor, this core is described as the "heel of evil," the most coarse and tough part of the body of evil. In order to overcome this, a divine messenger, with superhuman powers, is needed. This messenger will collect the spiritual power of the whole people and utilize it to overcome the aspect of evil that cannot be vanquished directly. He believed that the messiah, whom he identified as Shabbatai Zevi, was the incarnation of the sixth divine *sefirah*, *tifferet*, and that he came to the world for this purpose. Nathan proclaimed that each Jew should give the messiah spiritual force in the form of faith in him, and the messiah will then focus the powers of the whole people to achieve the final victory over the forces of evil. Thus, Nathan introduced into Judaism the concept of a mediated religious relationship with God, giving the messiah (for the first time in a millennium and a half) the role of being the intermediary between the worshipper and the supreme Godhead, and allotting to him a position of an incarnated divine power. He did that on the basis of kabbalistic concepts, and the wide approval these ideas enjoyed reflected the widespread influence of the kabbalah in the seventeenth century.

Nathan's theology of the messiah was the complete opposite of Lurianic teachings, even though he used Lurianic terminology and worldview. Luria and his disciples described a direct relationship between man and God, and viewed the *tikkun* as the involvement of every individual in the process of redemption—a most heavy burden that ordinary people found hard to undertake. Nathan, on the other hand, positioned the divine messiah in the middle, mediating between the worshipper and the task of the *tikkun*. Every Jew has to express his complete faith in the messiah; the Sabbatians often designated their creed by the term *"emunah"* (faith). The messiah transforms this spiritual power into a weapon to vanquish evil and redeem the universe.

The theological challenge facing Nathan of Gaza and other Sabbatian thinkers changed dramatically late in 1666, when Shabbatai Zevi was summoned to the palace of the Ottoman sultan. He emerged from the meeting wearing the Muslim cap. Having been threatened, Shabbatai Zevi did not hesitate for long before converting to Islam. Judaism was suddenly faced with a situation in which the messiah committed the worst possible sin that generations of Jews were educated to avoid. One has, when faced with a demand to convert, to become a martyr and "sanctify the holy name" rather then betray one's God, people, and tradition. Shabbatai Zevi, who should have been the example of religious perfection and who was regarded not only as a divine messenger but also as a divine incarnation, did the exact opposite.

Most Jewish historians in the nineteenth and early twentieth centuries regarded the conversion as the end of the Sabbatian movement, and described the groups of Sabbatians that continued to be active as "remnants," having no historical significance. It was Gershom Scholem who proved in several books and many studies that Sabbatian messianism continued to exert meaningful influence for the next 150 years, and that it contributed to the shaping of Jewish culture in modern times. Scholem explained that religions are not devastated by a historical paradox but rather thrive on it. The execution of the messiah as a common thief did not put an end to Christianity; it was actually its beginning. In a similar way, the paradox of a converted messiah was the beginning of a new religion within

Judaism, and sects of believers continued to thrive also within Islam and Christianity.

It was Nathan's task to explain the conversion to the believers. He insisted that his prophecy was true, and that the *tikkun* had indeed been completed and the age of redemption had actually begun. The conversion was explained as a necessary stage in the struggle against the continued resistance of the powers at the core of evil's realm. These powers cannot be vanquished from the outside: the messiah had to pretend to be one of them, to assume a disguise, in order to enter their realm and overcome them from the inside. One of the most fascinating and meaningful processes that occurred as a result of Shabbatai Zevi's conversion was the intense re-reading and re-interpreting of the ancient sacred texts—the Bible, the Talmud, and the Zohar—and the "discovery" of numerous verses and statements that indicate the necessity of the messiah's conversion to an "evil" religion.

It was an endeavor similar to that of the early Christians, who interpreted the writings of the ancient prophets of Israel as predicting the birth, life, death, and resurrection of Christ. Another example was the interpretation of the Bible and the Talmud by the early kabbalists, who discovered in every verse and rabbinic statement references to the system of the *sefirot* and the concept of the feminine *shekhinah*. The Sabbatian writers often referred to the same verses that Christian commentators used concerning the messiah, and some of their opponents pointed out the similarities between Sabbatian and Christian conceptions of the role of the messiah as an intermediary and the verses that were presented in support of these ideas. These similarities increased after Shabbatai Zevi's death in 1676, when both Sabbatians and Christians presented concepts of messianism in which the redemption had already occurred, and in which the messiah will return to signify the completion of the process. It is interesting to note that contemporary writers who find it very important to present links between the kabbalah and Christianity somehow tend to ignore the prominent and obvious phenomenological similarities between Sabbatianism and early Christianity.

Another aspect in which a close parallel between Sabbatianism and Christianity existed relates to the concept of the Torah and its commandments as presented by Nathan of Gaza. Using Lurianic terms indicating the various layers of existence, Nathan described the Torah as given by Moses and followed by Jews in all generations as the Torah reflecting the layer of "creation" (*torah de-beriah*). The Torah that is now taking its place is the Torah of the highest spiritual layer, that of divine emanations (*torah de-azilut*). The physical commandments, the numerous rituals, are all part of the lower stratum of the Torah. The higher one, the Torah of the messianic age, is spiritual in character, relating to faith and enlightenment rather than the subjugation of the body. The strange behavior of Shabbatai Zevi, culminating in his conversion, was a reflection of the higher, spiritual Torah. (The similarity between these ideas and the Pauline interpretation of the biblical commandments as relating to the premessianic era, and the idea that they should now be reinterpreted in a spiritual manner, is more than remarkable.) These concepts open the gate widely for antinomian commentaries on Jewish law. It was now possible to denounce the halakhah as relevant only to the unredeemed world, while new vistas of spiritual freedom were open for the believers.

Several thousands of Sabbatians followed Shabbatai Zevi in the last decades of the seventeenth century and converted to Islam. Their Turkish neighbors designated them as *doenmeh* (foreigners), and they continued their sectarian existence for centuries, to this very day. Most Sabbatians, however, remained within Jewish communities, and created an underground of believers in all strata of Jewish society, simple people, intellectuals, and rabbis. They imitated their messiah in a kind of "sacred hypocrisy": they pretended to be orthodox Jews, adhering to the ancient exilic tradition, while secretly they worshiped the messiah and the Torah of the age of redemption. They expressed this in various ways. A common one was to celebrate the birthday of the messiah, which occurred on the day of mourning and fasting for the destruction of the temple—*tisha'a be-Av*; when everybody was crying and praying they celebrated the end of the exile and the coming of the messiah.

We know of a score or more separate Sabbatian sects in Judaism in the late seventeenth century and throughout the eighteenth. Their teachings were diverse, as were their practices. There were several groups that traveled to Jerusalem to await the return of the messiah. Others assembled around leaders who claimed to be the heirs or reincarnations of Shabbatai Zevi. There was no central authority or organization, nor any normative theology. Several writers produced books relating visions and messianic experiences. Some groups were led by messianic figures, who were not directly related to the Sabbatian tradition. The existence of these heretical sects hiding in many communities evoked a reaction: there were several rabbis who dedicated themselves to the hunting and discovering Sabbatian believers and identifying books reflecting a Sabbatian worldview. A bitter controversy arose in the 1730s when the chief rabbi of Prague, a prominent scholar, Rabbi Jonathan Eibschutz, was accused of being a secret believer in Shabbatai Zevi—an accusation that modern scholarship has proved to be correct.

One of Scholem's main theses was the observation that this profound crisis that traditional Judaism was undergoing in the eighteenth century served as a basis for the emergence of the enlightenment movement in Judaism, which preached the integration of Jews in European society and culture. According to him, the walls of the Jewish ghettos in Europe fell down from within, before they were breached from the outside by the process of the emancipation of European Jews. The traditional norms lost their power under the onslaught of Sabbatian ideas, and prepared Jews for a new era of freedom and openness. This is a profound thesis, even though there are very few details that can be presented to prove it.

In the middle of the eighteenth century, Jacob Frank, a Pole who claimed to be a reincarnation of Shabbatai Zevi, presented a radical, heretical interpretation of the concept of the new, spiritual Torah. One of the slogans that he propagated was "the denial of the Torah is the true expression of adherence to it." Everything in traditional law has now to be reversed, and prohibitions are now positive commandments. Prohibited erotic behavior is demanded in the present, the age of the redemption. He developed a visionary, anarchistic worldview, which demanded the destruction of the present, unredeemed world to make way for the messianic one. His radical heresy horrified the rabbinic authorities of the Jewish communities, which excommunicated the sect, known as Frankists, in the strongest terms. Jacob Frank approached the Catholic Church in Poland and entered into a prolonged process of negotiations concerning the terms of the sect's conversion, insisting on keeping the sectarian structure of his believers. In this process the Frankists twice faced Jewish rabbis in disputations organized by the church, in 1757 and 1760; in the latter year Frank and several thousands of his adherents converted to Christianity. He established his court in Offenbach, near Frankfurt, and many of his believers became active in the European wars that followed the French Revolution. The Frankists were the most radical form of Jewish heresy, rebellious and destructive, and the most extreme example of antinomianism. The intensely orthodox doctrines of Isaac Luria had been turned in this case into a complete denial of Jewish laws and norms.

Some of the mystical messianic ideas developed in the various sects of the Sabbatians survived the decline of the movement at the end of the eighteenth century. They expressed, in different manners, several directions in which the kabbalah developed, the most important among them being the theology of the modern Hasidic movement, which is the most prominent expression of the kabbalah in contemporary Judaism.

8

Modern and Contemporary Hasidism

The kabbalistic tradition prevails in orthodox Judaism today within certain circles inside the Hasidic movement and among some of the movement's opponents. The schism between Hasidism and the *mitnagdim* (opponents) is the most significant historical phenomenon in modern Jewish traditional religious culture. It has characterized orthodox Judaism in the last two centuries, despite the great upheavals, catastrophes, and transformations that occurred during this period in Jewish life and destiny. In everyday English usage "Hasidim" often relates to all ultraorthodox Jews, ignoring, or perhaps unaware of, the conflict between Hasidim and the Opponents. In fact Jewish ultraorthodoxy in the United States, Israel, and Europe is divided about equally between Hasidim and Opponents sometimes called "Lithuanians," because that country was the center of the opposition to Hasidim in the eighteenth and nineteenth centuries. Despite the depth of this schism—so profound that marriages between adherents of the two factions are very rare—the groups are united in their fundamentally kabbalistic worldviews. The conflict can be conceived as one raging between two conceptions of the kabbalistic tradition. While the Opponents are essentially loyal to the Lurianic kabbalistic concepts, the Hasidim introduced some new concepts, especially concerning mystical leadership and messianism, into their version of the kabbalah.

11 The holy name of God should constantly be before the eyes of the
Hasid.

There is no basis, however, to the common misconception that the Opponents have a more "enlightened" and "rational" worldview, while the Hasidim are more inclined to indulge in kabbalah and mysticism. The leader of the Opponents in the late eighteenth century, Rabbi Eliyahu the Gaon of Vilna, was a kabbalist who wrote commentaries on several classics of this literature, and his disciples were immersed in traditional kabbalistic ideas and terminology. The concepts of God, the universe, and humanity as formulated by the Lurianic kabbalah still dominate the theologies of both the Hasidim and the Opponents.

Rabbi Israel Ba'al Shem Tov (1700–1760), who was known by the acronym Besht, founded the Hasidic movement in southern Russia. He was a kabbalist who wandered from place to place, preaching and serving as a healer and a magician. The movement took shape under the leadership of his main disciple, Rabbi Dov Baer of Mezheritch, who was known as the Great Magid, or preacher. Neither the Besht nor the Magid, who died in 1772, wrote books; their disciples collected and published their teachings. The Magid's teachings include an emphasis on the individual's communion with God (*devekuth*), and on introducing spirituality into the most mundane aspects of human life. The ideas of the Besht and the Magid and their followers were presented in a popular, exoteric language that avoided technical kabbalistic discourse; this gave the young movement an image of a popular, revivalistic spiritual phenomenon.

The young Hasidic movement was denounced and excommunicated in 1772 by the then great leader of rabbinic Judaism, Rabbi Eliyahu the Gaon of Vilna. This decree was renewed several times in subsequent decades and is still in force. It is probable that one of the reasons for this harsh treatment of the Hasidim by the rabbinic establishment of that time was the fear of a renewed eruption of Sabbatian heresy. Another was the fear that by emphasizing a mystical relationship with God, the Hasidim might weaken the adherence to the study of the Talmud, which was regarded as the supreme expression of spirituality in most eastern European communities.

Rabbi Dov Baer assembled around him a most unusual group of great teachers and charismatic leaders, who spread out after 1772 and established dozens of Hasidic communities throughout eastern Europe. These communities were modeled on the court of the Magid, and his teachings served as a starting point, though many of these disciples developed original and innovative religious and social conceptions. By the first decades of the nineteenth century, European Judaism was split between the Hasidim and their Opponents, often dividing communities into groups engaged in constant conflict. This situation prevails today in the orthodox Jewish centers in Israel and the United States. In most places they live in separate neighborhoods, keeping contact among them to a minimum. Despite this schism, both camps base their religious outlook on the teachings of the kabbalah, and many of their leaders write kabbalistic commentaries, treatises, and homiletical and ethical works.

Hasidic Dynasties and the Theory of the *Zaddik*

The teachings of the Besht and the Magid emphasized the centrality of communion with God, achieved especially by prayer, and the spiritual efforts required to correct evil and uplift it to its good, divine origins. Their main message was "there is no place from which He is absent," a kabbalistic panentheistic system. (While pantheism postulates that everything is God, panentheism claims that God is inside everything.) The movement, in its beginnings, was a pietist, spiritual one, including probably some messianic aspirations, led by charismatic preachers. Yet by the end of the eighteenth century, it evolved into a loose network of independent communities, each led by a *zaddik*, a mystical leader. Most of the founding fathers of these sects or communities were the charismatic disciples of the Magid. However, this mode of leadership was not continued after the first generation. The early leaders established dynasties (often known by their place of origin, little eastern European towns such as Bratslav, Liadi, and Belz), and leadership was transferred from father to son. The transition from charismatic to dynastic leadership was expressed by the paradoxical doctrine that stated "there is no *zaddik* but the son of a *zaddik*"; "*zaddik*" in Hebrew is a common, simple term, meaning righteous or charitable. It is absurd to suppose that there is no righteous person but the son of one; this is a clear indication that the term "*zaddik*" acquired a new, radically different meaning in the context of Hasidic leadership.

The main mystical doctrine of Hasidism became the theory of the *zaddik*, which basically asserts that it is only possible to approach God through the mediation of the *zaddik*, who is regarded as a divine messenger. The *zaddik* (popularly called rebbe) is responsible for redeeming the souls of his adherents, bringing their prayers before the throne of God, and ensuring that if they sin their repentance will be accepted. He is also responsible for his believers' health, fertility, and livelihood. In return, the Hasidim (adherents) owe him faith, which he uses as a source of spiritual power to achieve these goals, and they provide the worldly needs of the *zaddik* and his family. When he dies, his son (or, sometimes, son-in-law) becomes *zaddik*. Each dynastic house of *zaddikim*, of which there are scores, has a group of followers. These dynastic groups have been established now for seven or eight generations, overcoming the dispersions and persecutions of eastern European Jewry. After the devastation of the Holocaust, they reestablished their centers on new continents, especially in and around New York City in the United States and Jerusalem and Bney-Brak in Israel. These dynasties survive and flourish because of the deep belief in the mystical bond holding together the dynasty of the *zaddik* and the families of his followers. The conception of the *zaddik* as an intermediary between the worshipper and God has become, since the early nineteenth century, the main subject that separates the Hasidim from the Opponents and, actually, every other

Jewish denomination. To non-Hasidim, this doctrine seems to be heretical, because it endows a human being with divine attributes, and denies direct connection between an individual and God.

It is rather clear that the theory of the *zaddik* is a microreflection of the messianic theory of Nathan of Gaza, the prophet of the Sabbatian movement. The universal redeemer of Sabbatianism was substituted in Hasidism by a minor redeemer, whose authority is constricted by geography, chronology, and a distinct group of adherents, but the basic structure remains intact. The *zaddik*—who is responsible for the spiritual and material welfare of his community, which puts its faith in him—can be described as a minor messianic figure, bringing to his adherents a kind of minimal redemption. Typologically, it is somewhat similar to the structure of the Catholic Church, which promises the faithful a spiritual and physical well-being through its power as an intermediary between the faithful and God. Both of them marginalize universal, cosmic redemption, because of the constant presence of the divine emissary within this world. In this sense, Hasidism "neutralized" the messianic drive in Jewish religious actvity (a term Gershom Scholem introduced to characterize Hasidism), and in its place established the *zaddik* as an everyday redeemer and savior. The dynastic structure provides confidence that this state of affairs will continue in the future. Because of this conservative impulse, Hasidism was the main opponent to all Jewish movements in the nineteenth and twentieth century that were motivated by a quest for a better life, both material and spiritual. The Hasidim fiercely opposed not only any attempt at religious reform, but also the emigration of Jews to new countries, including America, South Africa, and the western European nations. They also opposed Jewish socialist movements, and especially they were the most ardent opponents of Zionism. Many Hasidic groups do not recognize the State of Israel, and regard it as a foreign government established by Jewish heretics. Despite these beliefs, the Holocaust, which made Jewish life in traditional Hasidic areas impossible, forced some Hasidim to relocate to the United States and Israel.

Hasidic Messianism

The Sabbatian roots of the *zaddik* doctrine become apparent when a *zaddik* steps out of line and claims to be the redeemer not only of his own dynastic community but of the people of Israel as a whole. The Hasidic dynasties coexist because of their understanding that each of them is responsible first and foremost to the families of their traditional adherents, much like dynastic monarchies. However, from time to time there emerges a *zaddik* who claims to be "the true *zaddik*," a messiah for everybody, for all times. Rabbi Nahman of Bratslav, the grandson of the Besht, made such a claim in 1805–1811, and he continues to have adherents to this day—more than 190 years after his death—who await his return as the ultimate messianic redeemer.

Marginalized by other Hasidic communities as a small, insignificant sect, the Bratslav believers were few, unorganized, and poor. Yet, because they denied the dynastic structure, they were open to everybody, and preached their ideas and distributed their books to all. Therefore, outsiders who were interested in Hasidism often met them first. For example, Martin Buber first approached Hasidism when he translated Rabbi Nahman's narratives into German. Because there is no leadership structure in the Bratslav sect, it serves today as a meeting place for "repentants," secular Jews who seek to rejoin tradition but who are unwilling to accept the strict orthodoxy of the established Hasidic dynasties. The Bratslav sect created a kind of bohemian, anarchistic spiritual group, which, in the last few years, sometimes prefers to describe itself as kabbalistic rather than Hasidic, conforming to the atmosphere and attitudes of contemporary spiritualists.

This phenomenon was repeated on a much larger scale in Brooklyn in the 1980s and 1990s under the leadership of Rabbi Menachem Mendel Shneersohn, the seventh and last leader of Habad (Lubavitch) Hasidism, a rich and highly organized Hasidic sect. Tens of thousands of Jews in the United States, Europe, and Israel believed in Shneersohn's messianic mission, and saw the first Gulf War as an indication of the apocalyptic, messianic era's arrival. Shneersohn died in 1994, at the age of ninety-two, yet many of his Hasidim still believe in his destiny and await his return.

Rabbi Shenur Zalman of Liadi founded Habad Hasidism in the last decades of the eighteenth century, and it quickly became one of the most popular and well-organized Hasidic dynasties. The original teachings of the founder and his disciples tended to be intensely mystical, calling the visible universe a delusion, and preaching the submersion of individual characteristics and desires in quest of a complete fusion with the divine "nothingness," the supreme Godhead. Despite this mysticism, Habad Hasidism acquired an image of being the more intellectual and learned sect among the Hasidic dynasties. The center of the sect was moved from place to place during the nineteenth and twentieth centuries, and it was one of the earliest to be established in New York City just before the Second World War and the Holocaust.

Menachem Mendel Shneersohn, the son-in-law of the previous leader, assumed office in 1950, and began a vast project of building an international organization of Habad communities that quickly spread and encompassed every country and city in which Jews lived. An elaborate system of Habad schools became one of the strongest educational systems in orthodox Judaism, and the fame and authority of Habad spread more widely than any Hasidic sect. At the heart of this endeavor was a Habad legend, which said that there will be seven Habad leaders in succession, and the seventh will be childless and he will be the messiah who will redeem the whole world. Needless to say, Shneersohn was the seventh, and he died without an heir.

As he was growing old, the messianic enthusiasm among his adherents increased, and peaked in the late 1980s and the early 1990s. After his death some of the Habad faithful tried to diminish the messianic aspect, but many still worship him, pray at his grave, and await his return and the completion of the messianic process. Meanwhile, like the Bratslav Hasidim, they are leaderless, "dead Hasidim" as their opponents call them. It is impossible to predict now how the vast structure of Habad will develop in the future, but it is clear that Shneersohn was the leader of a great Jewish messianic movement in the twentieth century. Shneersohn did not emphasize the kabbalistic aspect of the messianic doctrine that he headed, yet his followers wrote detailed kabbalistic commentaries on his writings and sermons.

Neo-Hasidim

Since the last decades of the nineteenth century, a literary and spiritual phenomenon—which was expressed by the emergence of collections of Hasidic narratives, tales, and epigrams in Hebrew and Yiddish—joined the margins of the Hasidic movement. Some of the material in these anthologies was authentic, including the hagiography that surrounded the figures of the Hasidic leaders, but most of it was not; it also included traditional Jewish folktales and selections from traditional works. These books gained popularity and were widely circulated, though they were read mainly by people outside of the Hasidic communities themselves. The phenomenon was, to a very large extent, an expression of nostalgia for traditional Jewish life that was felt by Jews who left the orthodox, Hasidic communities and were struggling to integrate in modern European societies. Gradually, a distinct "non-Hasidic Hasidism" emerged, and this became a meaningful Jewish cultural phenomenon especially after the Holocaust, expressing the wish to cherish the old Jewish world that was so brutally destroyed. Collections of Hasidic tales were translated into many languages, and Jews and non-Jews shared an admiration for a past that was characterized by universal values of spirituality and social justice, which was now lost.

The impact of this neo-Hasidic literature, as it was sometimes called, peaked in the 1960s and 1970s, in the United States and Israel. Preachers and secular speakers quoted "Hasidic" tales and anecdotes at every possible opportunity. The term "Hasidic" became a substitute for "Jewish," reflecting the idea that Hasidism was somehow more spiritual and noble than just Judaism. This fashionable trend seems to have subsided in the 1980s, when authentic Hasidism gained strength and became a meaningful political and social presence in Judaism, and not just a distant memory of an extinct past. Yet it seems that the need for a more spiritual and noble synonym for "Judaism" was still present, and from the 1990s to the present "Hasidim" was replaced by the term "kabbalah." When adherents of Habad or Bratslav Hasidism establish new circles and preach their doctrines today, they often prefer to use the term "kabbalah" rather than "Hasidism," both in Israel and in the United States.

Traditional kabbalah exists today mainly within the Hasidic communities. Hasidism, however, brought about a return of the kabbalah to its original esoteric place in Jewish culture, after it was popularized by Lurianism. The concept of the religious intermediary between man and God, the Hasidic leader, the *zaddik*, relegated creative study of the kabbalah to the leaders rather than to the followers. Hasidic popular literature, which consists mainly of collections of sermons, uses kabbalistic terminology, but the serious and creative study of the kabbalah is the domain of the *zaddik* and his circle of scholars.

9

Some Aspects of
Contemporary Kabbalah

The Jewish enlightenment movement of the eighteenth century changed the status of the kabbalah and the meanings of the term dramatically both within Judaism and in European culture. This movement, which in the nineteenth century also became associated with religious reform, rejected the kabbalah as an expression of the ignorance and superstition of the Middle Ages, and strove to present Jewish worldviews based mainly on rationalism and adherence to social ethics. Jewish scholars and historians, especially those associated with the German "science of Judaism," including Heinrich Graetz, described the kabbalah in the most derogatory terms. The kabbalah in Judaism was associated with orthodox Judaism, and was studied mainly among the Hasidim and the Opponents, and among Jewish scholars in the Middle East and North Africa. Modern Jewish institutions of higher learning did not find a place for the kabbalah in their curricula. There were a few exceptions. The great Hebrew poet, Hayyim Nachman Bialik, included the kabbalah in his project of assembling, editing, and publishing the treasures of Jewish tradition in a nonorthodox, modern Hebrew context. And, the Hebrew University of Jerusalem, founded in 1926, invited Gershom Scholem to study and teach kabbalah at its Institute of Jewish Studies.

12   Esther represents the Jewish feminine divine power, the *Shekhinah*.

In Europe, the rift between science and the occult widened, and the kabbalah was rejected by mainstream culture and thought and relegated to marginalized groups of esoterics and spiritualists. In the second half of the nineteenth century such a circle—the theosophical school of Madame Helena Blavatsky, which spread in Russia and western Europe—attained some influence. Similar groups abounded in France, Germany, and England. The writings of such groups derived a great deal from the esotericist writings of the Christian kabbalists, and became part of popular pseudoscientific culture. Some elements of the Christian kabbalah were included in some rituals of the Freemason movement, adding an aura of mystery and antiquity to its teachings. These writings also served as a basis, for instance, for the psychology of religion presented in some of Carl Gustav Jung's writings, integrated with many other disparate elements, especially Hindu myths and alchemical traditions. This atmosphere also served as background for the rapid spread of the golem legend in the early decades of the twentieth century. A brief history of the subject should, therefore, be included here.

The Golem

Hundreds of commentaries were written on the Sefer Yezira between the tenth century and the twentieth. Two of them—written in the early thirteenth century in Germany by writers who were unaware of the kabbalah, which at that time had only made its first strides in southern Europe—include a section that describes, in detail, how the theory of the alphabet presented in the ancient work can be utilized to create a living human being out of earth, breathing life into it by certain methods of reciting the Hebrew letters. A dozen medieval and early modern texts support the view that Abraham or another sage used the Sefer Yezira to create a human being. In modern times, this artificial creature was called golem, and it became one of the most popular and well-known "kabbalistic" characteristics in the twentieth century.

The identification of the Sefer Yezira as a recipe for the creation of a human being is derived not from the Sefer Yezira itself, but from two opaque statements in the tractate Sanhedrin in the Babylonian Talmud. In one statement it is related that the early-fourth-century sage Rava created a person; in the second, two sages (of the same period) were studying "the laws of creation" and created a "triple calf" that they ate for a celebration. Some commentators identified these "laws of creation" with the Sefer Yezira, thus presenting the possibility of viewing the work as the basic laws that enabled Abraham to create a human being. When the kabbalists adopted the Sefer Yezira, creating such a being seemed to be inherent in kabbalistic tradition. It should be pointed out, however, that hardly a handful of the hundreds of kabbalists who dealt with the Sefer Yezira expressed such a view, and narratives about such an endeavor became popular only in modern times.

It seems that the background of the two sentences in the Talmud (no other reference to the "laws of creation" is found in the many thousands of pages of the Talmud and midrashim) is a subject completely remote from the Sefer Yezira. It is a question that scientists in ancient times and the Middle Ages debated: Is it possible to create life artificially? Many thinkers—among them some important Islamic philosophers—answered this question in the affirmative. This problem can be viewed as a purely scientific one, without any religious implications; in the same way that a man can build a house a man can create life. No doctrine of any religion gave this power to God alone. In the same way, the practice is not necessarily magical, but was regarded as scientific. An Islamic story tells about Hay Ibn Yoqtan, a wondrous figure that was created by the forces of nature alone, by the sun and the wind shaping a figure out of earth. A Jewish scholar described the way a person can create life: Put a large stone on wet ground, and lift it several months later: thriving insects and worms will come to life under it. The talmudic sentences may have referred to this.

The term "golem" became prevalent in folktales only in the modern period, when some scattered narratives about sages and kabbalists appeared on the margins of Jewish popular hagiographical literature. Several stories about such a creature appeared in eastern Europe, but the first ones, which connected it to Prague and its rabbi, were not written earlier than the end of the eighteenth century. Some German writers picked up the motif at the end of the nineteenth century and the beginning of the twentieth. The subject became a center of attention only after the publication, in 1909, of a collection of fictional narratives by Judah Rosenberg. The stories told of the Prague rabbi MaHaRaL (an acronym for Our Teacher Rabbi Judah Loeb), who, in the second half of the sixteenth century and the beginning of the seventeenth, created a golem in order to serve him and to protect the Czech Jews from their enemies. Rosenberg, who emigrated from Poland to Canada in the 1930s, believed himself to be the spiritual heir of the MaHaRaL, and he attributed the magical powers utilized by the Prague rabbi to Sefer Yezira and the kabbalah. Numerous writers embellished these stories and they were translated into many European languages, thus constituting a major best seller of Hebrew origins in twentieth-century European culture. Short stories, novels, plays, and operas were written in which the golem was the central hero, mostly between 1905 and 1925, in German, Yiddish, Hebrew, French, and English. Like Frankenstein's monster and, later, the robot, the golem is an assistant and a servant, sometimes a savior, but there is always the threat of his powers getting out of control and of him becoming dangerous to his creator and the surrounding community.

The phenomenon of the golem contributed meaningfully to the portrayal of the kabbalah as an esoteric, mysterious, and powerful compendium of ancient magic. It was replaced several decades later by another product of Prague—Karl Chapek's robot, which was first presented in his 1921 play *RUR*. Frankenstein's monster and the robot were portrayed as scientists' creations, and their life force is electric current. The life force of the golem is the Hebrew alphabet, the secret name of God inserted under his tongue, or the word "truth," one of God's names, engraved on his forehead. (When the first Hebrew letter of "truth" is erased, it becomes "dead.") The legend of the golem conformed to, and strengthened, the image of the kabbalah as doctrine that could bring great benefits, but one that also includes some sinister, dangerous elements.

Twentieth-Century Thinkers

Among the most important Jewish thinkers of the twentieth century, there was one outstanding kabbalist in the traditional sense of the term. Rabbi Judah Ashlag, a Lurianic kabbalist, who worked in Jerusalem and Tel Aviv in the first half and the middle of the century, wrote an extensive commentary on all parts of the Zohar, presenting its teachings as being in harmony with those of Luria. His multivolume work includes the full translation of the Zohar to Hebrew. Other prominent thinkers did not present the kabbalah at the center of their published works. One of the most influential thinkers of the century, Rabbi Abraham Yitshak ha-Cohen Kook—who served as a chief rabbi of Palestine, under the British mandate, in the 1920s and the 1930s—presented in numerous works a new, revolutionary theology. This theology combined traditional orthodoxy with expectations of imminent redemption, for which, according to him, the Zionist endeavor is a vehicle. His language includes original terminology, expressed in intense poetic style. It is possible to interpret Rabbi Kook's writings as an attempt to present Lurianic teachings without using particular kabbalistic terminology. He relied extensively on medieval and modern philosophers, but some of his readers find behind these the basic ideas of Lurianism.

It is possible to detect a somewhat similar approach in the work of the great orthodox thinker of American Judaism, Rabbi Dov Baer Soloveitchik of Boston. He presented a modern conception of Judaism in the contemporary world, using the writings of Maimonides and modern philosophers as a starting point. Some of his readers suggest that here, too, there is an attempt to present kabbalistic ideas in contemporary, nonkabbalistic terminology. The kabbalah, and especially Hasidism, served as sources for some of the teachings of Martin Buber, who became the best-known twentieth-century Jewish thinker among modern Jews and non-Jews. His anthologies of Hasidic teachings became very popular and were translated to all major European languages.

The New Age

Since the 1970s, kabbalah became a central component of the fast-spreading New Age speculations and presentations. Numerous New Age works, mostly Christian, used the title "kabbalah" and claimed to possess secret knowledge derived from kabbalistic sources. The spread of the Internet in the last two decades has been particularly meaningful in this realm. Hundreds of Internet sites are dedicated to New Age–style presentations of various worldviews that claim to be kabbalistic. Most of them are Christian, but many of them are propagated by Jewish writers. Many of them serve groups and circles of adherents, spread all over the English-speaking world, and penetrating also German, French, and Italian popular culture. Most of the material on these sites is a combination of apocalyptic speculations, astrology, and alchemy; one of the central concepts attributed to the kabbalah is that of reincarnation of souls, and another is the cosmic harmony among the various aspects of the universe and the divine realm.

Some such trends assumed more systematic and structured expressions. Since the 1970s, an author who presented himself as Ze'ev ben Shimon Halevi has published a score of books dealing with various aspects of the kabbalah in London. Ze'ev ben Shimon Halevi is the pen name of Warren Kenton of Hampstead, who established several groups and circles who study his books in England. A more widespread organized phenomenon is the Center for the Study of Kabbalah, founded by Philip S. Berg in California in the 1970s, which is now a worldwide empire. Berg's starting point was the writings of Rabbi Ashlag; he translated portions of his Zohar commentary and other works, which were followed by his own works. This center achieved wide popularity among different social groups; at its core are some orthodox rabbis who strive to teach the traditional Jewish way of life to secularized Jews, but its centers and study groups attract all kinds of seekers of spirituality, many of them Christians. Most of their teachings adhere to the prominent aspects of New Age attitudes. Its Hollywood center presents many celebrities as adherents, the best known among them is Madonna, who adopted the name Esther, one of the kabbalistic appellations of the *shekhinah*, thus representing a physical union between the Virgin and the Jewish feminine divine power.

These and similar phenomena placed the term "kabbalah" in the center of the spiritual discourse in Western culture in the beginning of the twenty-first century. The meanings attributed to this term today are, in most cases, vastly different from those that prevailed in traditional kabbalah of the Middle Ages and early modern times. It is impossible at this early stage of these developing trends to present a balanced historical description. The kabbalah that appeared more than eight hundred years ago in medieval Europe and assumed various aspects and meanings throughout its history is still present, in dynamic and variegated forms, in the contemporary world.

Conclusion

Contemporary readers may meet the term "kabbalah" mostly in the following contexts; in each of them, the term conveys a different meaning:

1) In a scholarly-historical context, it is an important aspect of Jewish religious thought, which also includes

many of the mystical phenomena in Judaism. The term "kabbalah" in this context appeared at the end of the twelfth century, in the Book Bahir and the Provence circle; reached its medieval peak in the Zohar; and was renovated and reinvigorated in Safed to become the dominant aspect of Jewish spirituality. Its ideas have been integrated with Jewish messianism and have motivated the Sabbatian and other movements, and its terminology is utilized today by the Hasidic movement. The key terms by which it is recognized are the system of ten *sefirot*, the divine tree, and the feminine power in the divine realm, the *shekhinah*.

2) In the context of European religious and intellectual history, the kabbalah is conceived as an ancient, mysterious, occult doctrine, preserved in Jewish texts and integrated into Christian theology and European philosophy and science by a Florentine school of Renaissance thinkers. Between the end of the fifteenth and the eighteenth centuries, scores of prominent European scholars integrated it with esoteric speculations, science, and magic. It has been deeply associated with astrological, numerological, and alchemical speculations, and merged with the conceptions of a multilayered harmonious universe that characterize European modern esotericism.

3) The term "kabbalah" has been used often by esoteric circles of European spiritualists, theosophists, psychologists, and occultists, from Madame Blavatsky to Carl Jung, who often identified it with magic in the nineteenth and early twentieth century.

4) In contemporary orthodox Judaism, kabbalah is a central subject in the works of leaders and teachers of various Hasidic communities, and some groups of adherents

study it in a traditional manner (mainly the Zohar and the wriitngs of Rabbi Hayyim Vital). An important contribution to twentieth-century study of kabbalah is Rabbi Judah Ashlag's multivolume commentary to the Zohar.

5) In contemporary Israel there are numerous groups and circles that describe themselves as kabbalistic. Some of them are related to exoteric Hasidic groups, especially those of Bratslav and Habad (Lubavitch). Another contemporary Israeli usage is the tendency of magicians and popular healers to designate themselves as kabbalists.

6) A wide variety of groups and movements, Jewish and Christian, associated with the New Age phenomenon also use the term. They range from orthodox Jewish groups, such as the Center for the Study of Kabbalah, to nonorthodox Jewish seekers of a more spiritual Judaism to mainstream Christian New Age writings, which often identify the kabbalah with magic, alchemy, and astrology. In this context the kabbalah is conceived as universal phenomenon, and it seems that today it is the most potent and dominant usage to the term "kabbalah," despite the wide variety of meanings attached to it. Its historical contours cannot yet be clearly defined.

Further Reading

Bibliography

Dan, Joseph, and Esther Liebes, eds. *The Catalogue of the Gershom Scholem Library in Jewish Mysticism*, vols. 1 and 2. Jerusalem: National and University Library, 1999. Arranged by periods, schools, and main subjects in the history of Jewish mysticism, this work includes more than twenty thousand books and treatises, studies and reviews, making it the most comprehensive general bibliography concerning Jewish mysticism.

General Studies

Dan, Joseph. *Jewish Mysticism*, vol. 3: *General Characteristics and Comparative Studies*. Northvale, NJ: Aronson, 1999.
Dan, Joseph. *The Heart and the Fountain*. New York: Oxford University Press, 2002.
Dan, Joseph. *Gershom Scholem and the Mystical Dimension in Jewish History*. New York: New York University Press, 1986.
Green, Arthur, ed. *Jewish Spirituality, vols. 1 and 2.* New York: Crossroads, 1986–1987.
Idel, Moshe. *Kabbalah: New Perspectives*. New Haven, CT: Yale University Press, 1989.

Idel, Moshe. *Messianic Mystics*. New Haven, CT: Yale University Press, 1998.

Jacobs, Louis. *Jewish Mystical Testimonies*. New York: Schocken, 1996.

Scholem, Gershom. *Major Trends in Jewish Mysticism*. New York: Schocken, 1954. Scholem's work includes chapters devoted to ancient Jewish mysticism, Abraham Abulafia, the Zohar, Safed and Luria, Sabbatianism, and Hasidism.

Scholem, Gershom. *On the Kabbalah and Its Symbolism*. New York: Schocken, 1965. Includes articles on the concept of the Torah and the golem.

Scholem, Gershom. *On the Mystical Shape of the Godhead*. New York: Schocken, 1993. Discusses the *shekhinah* and the nature of good and evil.

Scholem, Gershom. *Jewish Messianism and Other Essays*. New York: Schocken, 1973. Covers Sabbatianism and Hasidism.

Scholem, Gershom. *Kabbalah*. Jerusalem: Keter, 1974. This volume contains the author's articles on Jewish mysticism found in the *Encyclopedia Judaica*.

Ancient Jewish Mysticism

Dan, Joseph. *The Ancient Jewish Mysticism*. Tel Aviv: MOD, 1993.

Dan, Joseph. *Jewish Mysticism, vol. 1: Late Antiquity*. Northvale, NJ: Aronson, 1998.

Halperin, David. *The Faces of the Chariot*. Tübingen, Germany: Mohr Siebeck, 1988.

Hayman, Peter. *Sefer Yesira: Edition, Translation, and Text-Critical Commentary*. Tübingen, Germany: Mohr Siebeck, 2004.

Schaefer, Peter. *The Hidden and Manifest God: Some Major Themes in Early Jewish Mysticism*. Albany: State University of New York Press, 1992.

Schaefer, Peter. *Synopse zur Hekhalot-Literatur*. Tübingen, Germany: Mohr Siebeck, 1981. These are the original Hebrew texts as found in seven key manuscripts.

Scholem, Gershom. *Jewish Gnosticism, Merkabah Mysticism and Talmudic Tradition*. 2nd ed. New York: Jewish Theological Seminary, 1965.

Early Kabbalah

Dan, Joseph, and Ronald Keiner. *The Early Kabbalah*. New York: Paulist Press, 1987. Part of the Classics of Western Spirituality series, this volume includes translations from early kabbalistic treatises.

Dan, Joseph. *Jewish Mysticism, vol. 2: The Middle Ages*. Northvale, NJ: Aronson, 1998.

Kaplan, Aryeh. *The Bahir*. Northvale, NJ: Aronson, 1995. Kaplan offers a translation and commentary on this important work.

Idel, Moshe. *The Mystical Experience in Abraham Abulafia*. Albany: State University of New York Press, 1988.

Scholem, Gershom. *The Origins of the Kabbalah*. Ed. R. J. Zwi Werblowsky. Princeton, NJ: Princeton University Press, 1987.

Wolfson, Elliot. *Through a Speculum that Shines: Visions and Imagination in Medieval Jewish Mysticism*. Albany: State University of New York Press, 1994.

The Zohar

Liebes, Yehudah. *Studies in the Zohar*. New York: State University of New York Press, 1993.

Matt, Daniel C. *The Zohar: Translation and Commentary*, vols. 1 and 2. Stanford, CA: Stanford University Press, 2004. Arthur Green provides the introduction.

Matt, Daniel C. *The Zohar: English Selection*. New York: Paulist Press, 1983.

Tishby, Isaiah. *The Wisdom of the Zohar*, vols. 1 and 2. Trans. D. Goldstein. Oxford: Oxford University Press, 1989. Includes an anthology of sections from the Zohar arranged according to subject, with detailed commentary.

The Christian Kabbalah

Dan, Joseph, ed. *The Christian Kabbalah*. Cambridge, MA: Harvard University Press, 1997.

Reuchlin, Johannes. *De arte cabbalistica*. Trans. Martin and Sarah Goodman. Lincoln: University of Nebraska Press, 1993.

Safed and Luria

Fine, Lawrence. *Safed Spirituality: Rules of Mystical Piety*. New York: Paulist Press, 1984.

Fine, Lawrence. *Physician of the Soul, Healer of the Cosmos: Isaac Luria and His Kabbalistic Fellowship*. Stanford, CA: Stanford University Press, 2003.

Werblowsky, R. J. Zwi. *Joseph Karo: Lawyer and Mystic*. Oxford, England: Oxford University Press, 1962.

The Sabbatian Movement

Liebes, Yehudah. *Studies in Jewish Myth and Messianism*. Albany: State University of New York Press, 1993.

Scholem, Gershom. *Sabbatai Sevi: The Mystical Messiah, 1626–1676*. Princeton, NJ: Princeton University Press, 1973.

Hasidism and the Modern Period

Band, Arnold. *The Stories of Rabbi Nahman of Bratslav*. New York: Paulist Press, 1978.

Buber, Martin. *The Tales of the Hasidim*. New York: Schocken, 1991.

Dan, Joseph. *Jewish Mysticism, vol. 4: The Modern Period*. Northvale, NJ: Aronson, 1999.

Dan, Joseph. *The Teachings of Hasidism*. New York: Behrman, 1983.

Elior, Rachel. *The Paradoxical Ascent to God: The Kabbalistic Theosophy of Habad Hasidism*. Albany: State University of New York Press, 1993.

Green, Arthur. *Tormented Master: The Life of Rabbi Nahman of Bratslav*. University: University of Alabama Press, 1979.

Rapoport-Albert, Ada, ed. *Hasidism Reappraised*. London: Vallentine Mitchel, 1996.

Uffenheimer, Rivkah Schatz. *Hasidism as Mysticism: Qietistic Elements in Eighteenth-Century Hasidic Outlook*. Princeton, NJ: Princeton University Press, 1993.

Index